LENTEN LANDS

In 1953 a little American boy arrived in England with his mother and brother. He was the child of two dynamic and gifted parents, and his early years had not been without turbulent moments; but he did not know the extraordinary directions his life would take.

For his mother was Joy Davidman, who was to become the wife of C. S. Lewis. Here we learn the moving story of their relationship, seen through the child's eyes. With the growing boy we gain fresh insights into life at The Kilns, the Oxford-shire home that C. S. Lewis shared with his brother, Warnie, and his newly acquired family.

Remember
HELEN JOY
DAVIDMAN

D. July 1960

Loved wife of
C. S. LEWIS

Here the whole world (stars, water, air,
And field, and forest, as they were
Reflected in a single mind)
Like cast off clothes was left behind
In ashes, yet with hopes that she,
Re-born from holy poverty,
In lenten lands, hereafter may
Resume them on her Easter Day.

LENTEN LANDS

Douglas Gresham

HarperSanFrancisco
A Division of HarperCollins*Publishers*

First published in hardcover in the USA in 1988
by the Macmillan Publishing Company,
New York, and in Great Britain in 1989 by
William Collins Sons & Co. Ltd.

Gresham, Douglas H.
Lenten lands / Douglas Gresham.
p. cm.
Previously published: New York: Macmillan, 1988.
Includes index.
ISBN 0-06-063447-2 (pbk.)
1. Lewis, C. S. (Clive Staples), 1898-1963—Family.
2. Authors, English—20th century—Family
relationships. 3. Authors, English—20th
century—Biography. 4. Gresham, Douglas H.
—Childhood and youth. 5. Davidman, Joy—
Family. I. Title.
[PR6023.E926Z665 1994]
929'.2'0973—dc20   94-4366

94 95 96 97 98   10 9 8 7 6 5 4 3 2 1

To this collection of memories,
I wish to add one more small memory.
I knew her for a very short time,
but in that time grew to love her,
surprisingly deeply. So this book is
dedicated to the memory of Erika Dorsett,
for Erika died suddenly at 5:45 A.M. on
the 2nd of February, 1983, at the age of ten.
I too loved "Who."

CONTENTS

PREFACE

It has taken me a long time to write this book; in a sense you could say that it has taken twenty years. For much of that time I have been reluctant to talk about the experiences of my childhood and youth, partly because the old wounds still ache, and never more so than when under discussion; but more from an inward sense of privacy that I learnt from my stepfather (C. S. Lewis) and my uncle (W. H. Lewis). A third reason for remaining silent has been an unwillingness to join the burgeoning C. S. Lewis bandwagon. This book is not primarily a book about C. S. Lewis; it is a book about D. H. Gresham.

I have finally written my story for a variety of reasons; the first of which is that I was asked to do so. In 1982, I was approached by Lyle Dorsett, who was embarking on the difficult and demanding task of writing a biography of my mother, Joy Davidman, a task which he performed ably, as witnessed by his book *And God Came In*. Lyle wanted to talk with me about my recollections of my mother and her years with both my father, a novelist, W. L. Gresham, and with my stepfather, C. S. Lewis. Because I live in Tasmania, an island situated about 250 miles off the south-eastern corner of Australia, there were obvious difficulties involved in our getting together. Eventually these were overcome by the good offices of the people at the Marion E. Wade Center of Wheaton College, in Illinois, who sponsored my visit to Wheaton in return for a videotape of Lyle's interview with me. From a transcript of that tape has grown this book, a process which Lyle Dorsett suggested I undertake, and in which he was supported by Peter Veltman, who was at that time interim Curator of the Wade Center. (Lyle Dorsett has since been appointed Curator.)

Another reason for writing down my memories is that over the years several misconceptions have arisen concerning my stepfather, and if I can correct any of these it is probably my duty to do so. I have heard, for example, members of several churches proclaim that "of course C. S. Lewis was one of us." In fact C. S. Lewis was a Christian not given to "isms," and whilst he preferred to attend the local Anglican church, this was more a matter of convenience than of conviction. It was from him that I learnt that Sectarianism is one of the Devil's keenest weapons against Christendom. It is also evident that some writers regard his relationship with my mother as, at best, a passing aberration, or as, at worst, evidence of his personal weakness. It was in fact the climax of everything that his earthly life had led up to, and his life after her death was merely an exercise in patience and obedience.

Finally to write all this down has been a therapeutic procedure for me. The ghosts, and the fears they engender, which have been locked firmly away in the deepest dungeons of my mind for twenty years have all been let, limping, out into the sunlight of objectivity for examination. As a result of this exercise I have realised that my childhood was not a time of testing and torment, but a privilege, a gift of education and experience greater than some of us gain in a lifetime.

LENTEN LANDS

CHAPTER 1

Me

THE CANDLE FLAME stood tall and unmoving, creating its own small pool of light in the darkness which seemed to surround me. I saw almost nothing else; the candle, the coffin upon which it stood and the low overhanging branches of the yew tree which were to shelter the grave. I stood staring down at the coffin until the Vicar moved directly in front of me to perform the ritual which would bring to a definite end the second part of my life. Father Head said his words, and the coffin was lowered gently into the earth by men whose faces were revoltingly impassive, smooth and professionally respectful. How I loathe funerals! On that day in November 1963 there was a bitter stillness about the world; for the second time in my life everything I knew, everything I held dear and the one person I loved had been swept away.

At that point I had no parents, no home and no hope. The winding path of life that had led me to this place and this time had provided strange contrasts and strange similarities in the pattern of my environments. There was always a House, for example; not just a house though, but a distinctive house, one which stood out from its neighbours, different and aloof although neglected and sadly in need of repair. In America, my father's, W. L. Gresham's, choice was a tall, gracious, white, pillared structure of three

3

stories. In England, my stepfather, C. S. Lewis, lived in a two-floor red brick monstrosity which had grown more by accident than by design. I loved both these homes. There were other parallels, too; there was always a lake. The Endekill Brook, in upstate New York, was dammed by a small wall of stones and formed a wide pool. In Oxford there was a disused clay-pit in the wood, deep and still, filled with the strange mystery that still water and its denizens seem to weave about themselves. Then there was the wood itself, the trees so alike and yet so different. Pines in rows in Staatsburg, broken here and there by dogwoods and maples. In Headington there were sycamores, oaks, birches and beeches all mixed together in the higgledy-piggledy fashion so typical of an English wood, and at the top of the hill a grove of larches. I was always surrounded by books, too, books and writers, and the wide and lively conversation which seem to be their hallmark. My stepfather's funeral really was the beginning of many things as well as the end of so many others, and I am beginning to realise that every point in one's life at which one loses everything is far more a beginning than an end, for one has lost merely the past, and one has yet to gain the future, and eternity itself. On that morning, the 26th of November, 1963, I was just eighteen years old.

I was born on the 10th of November, 1945, in the city of New York. The Gresham family then consisted of my father, William Lindsay Gresham, my mother, Helen Joy Davidman Gresham, my brother, David Lindsay Gresham and myself. At some stage during the first two years of my life, the family moved to Ossining, New York, where we lived for a while. Of that time I have no memories.

My first recollections are of the beautiful house and

estate at Endekill Road, Staatsburg, New York (about seventy-five miles north of New York City), and of the forests and fields which surrounded it; dark, cool pines, welcoming gentle dogwoods and majestic, towering maples lent their shade and their beauty to my childhood. I first remember being alive at about the time that I was three years old, and the Staatsburg home was a heaven for a little boy, teaching from the very beginning the meaning of beauty. Hot summers, the long dusty days frequently split apart by electrical storms with awesome power of sound and spectacle, dramatic autumns as the maples changed from silent dark greens to mellow gold and then to shrieking soprano reds before dying away through vermilion to brown and finally sighing into the annual little death that, for trees, is winter. The thick blanket of snow which brought the sleep of winter to the woods and meadows brought delight and excitement to a child, as well as sleds, toboggans, snowmen and snowball fights and the quiet, strangely holy, snowbound Christmas. For the little boy who became me, winter meant just two things: snow first and then Christmas, the one leading as if by decree to the other. And then, after Christmas, one simply waited for the thaw and the riotous exuberance of spring, as the sleeping world exploded into vibrant glowing life. I loved that place, and there live within me still the shocks of one or two incidents so breathtaking that the very memory of them even now seems to stop the world. Standing, for example, on the first-floor balcony of the large, decaying mansion that was our home and looking down into the heavy, warm darkness of a summer evening to see a carpet six or seven feet deep of millions of fireflies. They flew about three feet from the ground at the lowest to about ten feet up and appeared as a layer of flashing, winking, starlike lights. Once I came face to face with a doe and her fawn in the forest, and it would be hard to say who was the more frightened! A wonderful place for a little boy to grow, but all worldly Edens have their serpents, and mine was no exception. Outside, in the kindliness of nature, the world of this early part of my childhood was mostly a peaceful, fascinating land of many delights and some good and healthy terrors, snapping turtles and copperheads, for example, but indoors, as I passed from the age of three on towards six and then seven, things became very different and a strange and frightening change became apparent, even to a child as young as I was.

My father was a novelist and a writer of considerable talent. He had two major successes, *Nightmare Alley* and *Limbo Tower*. Both sold well, and *Nightmare Alley* was bought by a film company and then filmed, with Tyrone Power playing the lead. Dad's success with these two books made him a great deal of money and probably led him into the belief that he was destined to be a successful novelist for the rest of his career. He bought the estate at Staatsburg, "the Farm," as he loved to call the place, and a couple of saddle horses to go with it. I can still recall trying to walk in his bedroom, my entire legs encased in his bejewelled white cowboy boots. A fall resulting in a broken arm soon saw the end of the riding days and a fall at the hands of the Internal Revenue Service was soon to spell the end of the country-gentleman days. My father was a warm, loving man and he seems to remain mostly in my memory with a welcoming smile on his face and his arms widespread with open affection. I still can feel his bristly chin on my face; he would sit me on his lap and tell his jokes and tall tales, shaking with laughter. All of this was to change.

The woods and the meadows were to become a refuge from a house filled with mystifying currents of hard, brittle emotion; tension, fear and anger. The love and warmth of

shared fun and foolishness began to fade away. Mother and
Father began to talk more and more about "Income Tax."
Dad began to drink more and more heavily and would fly
into uncontrolled rages for little or no reason. Dianetics
emerged and became a topic for conversation in our
household. Dianetics is the name given to a system developed by an American science-fiction writer, one L. Ron
Hubbard, of self-help in the treatment of neurosis and
psychosis; it has been extended into a quasi-religious cult,
but seems to have no genuine basis in the light of current
psychiatric practise. Dad's stability and behaviour were
certainly much worse after his sessions of Dianetics than
they were before. I believe that experimentation with this
pseudo-science did a great deal of harm to the relationship
between my father and mother, already strained by a
multitude of factors, including financial problems, Dad's
sexual morality (unconventional for the time, in that he did
not believe that sexual infidelity was in any way wrong) and
perhaps most important Mother's undoubted ability as a
writer, her wide and agile mentality and her immense
innate intelligence, all of which must have made her a
difficult person for Dad to live with, for he shared many of
these characteristics.

When Dad drank, he drank heavily. He became vola-
tile, his temper explosive; he would roar around the house,
uncontrollable and at times dangerously violent. Once he
broke a bottle over my head; he smashed to matchwood a
good guitar when he repeatedly failed to master a difficult
run. I can remember the porch chairs being reduced to
small pieces against the pillars at the front of the house. For
me, the house became slowly but inevitably a place of
tension; the dusty, interesting attics changed from places
for exploration and adventure to rooms of forbidding
aspect, peopled by imaginary bogles and closed by invisible

bright barriers of impenetrable nothing, with only the swarming and now malevolent specks of dust falling and floating through mocking floods of sunlight. Anywhere on the farm, in the woods or down at the creek, was safe. Oh, there were fears enough, the breaking of a branch in a tree, falling into the Endekill Brook, or seeing a huge snake, but they were brief surges of clean terror and soon fled. Inside the house was a sick, constant uneasiness, an awareness that nastiness lurked. There was one place in the house where I felt completely safe and I spent considerable time there, securely protected from Dad's roaring and storming and immune to all the monsters which lurk in a child's imagination. The world might end around me, but I was safe and sound and invulnerable deep under the covers in my bed, for there I could hold my fear of my father and my love for him in about equal proportions.

Memories of Mother at that time are vague. She was big, warm and soft and cuddly. She was also busy, always busy. After the first few luxurious sprees, taxes and back taxes took their heavy toll and the family settled into a gentle poverty. Mother grew an acre or more of vegetables every year to help keep us all well fed. She also became an expert on wildwoods foods, gathering plants and fungi and rendering them into delicious dishes, albeit sometimes to the extreme apprehension of visiting friends. On walks in the woods Mother might suddenly cry "Aha!" and pounce upon a vile and evil-looking excresence of fungal growth to all appearances dripping with noxious yellow poison and gather an apronful of the stuff; then, without further comment on it, she would resume both the walk and the conversation. After a while her visitor would, with feigned nonchalance, make the awaited enquiry: "Ah . . . Joy?" Mother, all innocence, "Yes?" "Ah . . . er . . . uh, just what is all that yellow stuff?" Mother, with malice aforethought, "Supper!" She would, however, relent after watching her guest splutter and cough, obviously envisioning his or her forthcoming agonising death from fungal poisoning, and explain that the bright yellow funnelled fungi in her apron were the mushroom *Cantharellus cibarious*, better known as chanterelle, long famed as a delicacy in France and throughout most of south-western Europe. The name came from the Latin, *Cantharellus* being a diminutive of *cantharus*, from the Greek *kantharos*, which described a drinking vessel. Thus the delicate shape of the chanterelle was the reason for its name, although of course its flavour was of equal delicacy. This address would be delivered with such authority and obvious knowledge that guests always were willing to try the dish and usually enjoyed it. Mother really did know; no-one was ever poisoned. We gathered poke-weed (genus *Phytolacca*), which, when very young in its leafy stage, looks, cooks and tastes somewhat like spinach, but becomes toxic as it matures. Help came also from Mr. and Mrs. Jack Keator, who rented the farm buildings from us and ran a thriving chicken farm. They kept us well supplied with chickens and eggs. We ate a lot of chickens and eggs. Mother worked in the garden, picked fruit in the orchard, wrote in her study and somehow managed to feed her family and care for a somehow self-renewing torrent of cats, dogs, turtles, pet snakes and goodness only knows what else.

I can remember happy times at that home; going out into the forest in the deep snow to find a suitable tree to decorate for Christmas. Every tree examined had some flaw until finally we found it, *the* tree! Dragged home on a sled, it would be carefully erected in the living room and then with extreme artistry the myriad glittering glass balls and sparkly things would be placed, each one in a position thought out and discussed, so that it harmonised in colour and balance with every other decoration on the tree. The real secret of Christmas-tree decoration is to start by placing lots of lights in the tree. First, in close to the trunk, and then further out, until the last few are hanging right on the tips of the branches. If tinsel ropes or strings are used, they should come next and be placed inside the tree, mostly concealed by the outer ends of the branches, so that they are not obtrusive, but suddenly glitter and glow when the lights are turned on. Next, the glass balls and other little doo-dads; my personal preference is for the calm dignity of simple one-colour glass hangers of either spherical or teardrop shapes in as wide a variety of colours as possible. Then, if available, the good old-fashioned tinsel strips made of heavy foil, which will hang straight down when looped over the branches, resembling long, thin icicles. In my childhood days at Staatsburg, Dad would always finish the tree with one of those wonderful American ideas, which was called "Angel Hair." He would don a heavy pair of rubberised gauntlets and, with great care and finesse, spread this exquisitely fine spun-glass fibre amongst the branches. It was dangerous stuff to handle, but it made the tree look as if it were lightly covered with glowing white snow. Christmas was a special time for our family, and Dad was always far more generous with presents than he could afford to be. We would waken as early as possible on Christmas Day and rush downstairs to open and chortle with glee over our new toys.

I try to remember fairly and objectively those early days of my time, but I am forced to admit that I was happiest when alone with Mother, or just alone. By myself, I could gather and eat wild strawberries, play imaginary games and generally revel in the joys of being a little boy.

Sometime around this stage in my life, a shadowy insubstantial influence began to appear. It grew and gained in strength and solidity. Mother was philosophically and spiritually travelling through the long tunnel which leads from angry atheism through bewildered agnosticism out into the huge dim cavern of admission of the existence of God, thence to emerge blinking and blinded by the full light of Christianity, that sudden revelation for which our human tongues have no words of description. The name C. S. Lewis began to be heard in conversations between Dad and Mother, along with Income Tax, Dianetics, God and Senator McCarthy. My memories of this last are merely of an angry, ugly face which constantly reappeared in the newspapers.

There was much joy in those years at Staatsburg and considerable pain also. But all things come to an end, nothing lasts forever; the happiest joys and the deepest sorrows all have their endings. Being a little boy in itself is a transient occupation. The highs and lows of life at Staatsburg were not to last for long.

Dad and Mother (although they probably didn't know it and I certainly didn't) were already progressing along separate and slowly diverging orbital paths, like two comets briefly coming together in close proximity and travelling together for a while in companionship, generating a couple of small mischievous meteorites and then gradually drifting apart, their short liaison inevitably at an end. The days of watching with delight the arrival each summer of the fireflies and the first joyous snowfall each winter were inexorably running out. Outside influences were invading our family.

Dianetics, I believe, had a very destructive influence on Dad's personality. Mother's reading of the works of C. S. Lewis and becoming a convinced Christian certainly changed her. For me, life was getting better and better, for Mother had introduced us to Narnia and bedtime readings brought King Peter and Aslan into my world, or perhaps transported me to theirs.

As early as 1951, the structure of the Gresham family had begun to decay. I can remember that Mother was working very hard on the initial research for a book that was to become *Smoke on the Mountain*. In addition, she must also have been fraught with worry and anxiety about all the problems with which she was faced, our poverty and tax debts, Dad's drinking and his (to her) inexplicable infidelities and her own development as a Christian. The continued strain took its inevitable toll, and in 1952 Mother became ill, very ill. I remember her vomiting again and again into a large waxed cardboard container of the kind we used to store food in rented freezer space. I think hepatitis is the most likely diagnosis, looking back. In any case, Dr. Fritz Cohen, who was our family physician, came to the house and said that Mother was severely jaundiced and must be taken at once to the hospital. One picture remains like a frozen frame from a movie stuck fast in my mind— Mother emerging from her upstairs study wrapped in blankets. Mother's hair was black and she always wore it tied up in a bun on the back of her head. On this occasion, however, I saw her with her hair down, for the first time, and, to the best of my memory, for the last time also. It was a surprise to see that she had long, luxuriant hair down to her waist. I had not known, and had never stopped to think, what went to make up that bun on the back of her head.

Apparently, Fritz Cohen also recommended that upon her release from hospital, Mother should plan a complete rest, a change of environment and preferably a long vacation. It was here, at this point in 1952, that the plot began, not to thicken so much, but to convolute.

CHAPTER 2

Renée

RENÉE RODRIGUEZ, my mother's first cousin, was a stunningly beautiful girl. She had, during the time of their childhood, often floated into her cousin Joy's family circle and then out again, as an appendage of her determinedly socialite mother. Her childhood was about as fragmented and unhappy as that of most of the protagonists of this history. Renée had hastily and youthfully married a man from Alabama named Claude Pierce. Claude was a dashing young man full of Southern charm and his winning ways quickly swept Renée off her feet. They were married just in time to bid each other farewell, when Claude departed for Europe with George Patton's Third Army. Claude remained in battle in Europe almost continuously for eleven months, through the Battle of the Bulge and on eventually to that hellish conflagration the Battle of Berlin. When Claude returned, the gay, laughing Southern cavalier did not; he had become a dark, brooding character, jumpy and irritable, given to sudden bursts of temper. Claude never talked of his wartime experiences, or at least never to Renée; he never told her of the horrors he had seen and done, but, to her, he was obviously haunted and stricken. On his first night home, he rose in his bed with Renée, mumbling in his sleep, a phantom machine gun shaking his hands and arms with its nightmare recoil.

Claude would not, or possibly could not, talk about his terrors; he drank instead. The Pierce family, it seems, had been "shinny-makers" for generations, and Claude continued the family tradition, distilling his own "moonshine" or "white lightnin'." Renée found that from a promising career as a model, she had been relegated to a wife of the "barefoot and pregnant" type living just outside Mobile, Alabama. When Claude's friends were around, Renée was told to shut her mouth and stay in the kitchen out of the way. Amazingly, Renée put up with Claude's degrading her for a long time, but she had borne this man two children, Bob and Rosemary, and, at least at first, she loved him. However, as Claude became more and more deeply immersed in the vicious circle of self-pity, alcoholism and neurosis, he became steadily more brutal and violent. Completely unable to find any meaning or importance in the trivialities of everyday life after spending a year in a savage kill or be killed environment, resentful of the ingratitude of the world towards one who had suffered so much on its behalf, Claude, incapable of coping, simply slid further into a morass of problems, the outward manifestation of which was that he became a danger to live with.

Renée began to fear for her life and the safety of her children. Claude gave her little or no money, probably suspecting that she would leave if she was given half a chance, and eventually this became exactly what was in Renée's mind. But how to accomplish it? Obviously, to flee with two small children, penniless and on foot, was out of the question. Renée put her desperate and agile mind to work and devised a foolproof means of escape. She contacted her mother in secret and arranged for her to cable from New York to say that she was sick and needed Renée to take care of her. Renée told Claude that to make things easier for him, she would take the two children with her to her mother's place. Claude grudgingly allowed them to leave, and Renée accomplished the first part of her flight. Renée and Bob and Rosemary went to stay with Renée's mother, Rose, and after a while Renée gathered her courage around her and told Claude·on the phone that she was not returning to Mobile or to him. Perhaps Renée felt that she was safe in Manhattan and that Claude would not be able to reach her there. However, his reaction was to fry the phone line with some fairly powerful Southern self-expression and to inform Renée that he was coming to get her and that he would "kill any son of a bitch who got in his way." Renée was terrified and rushed to her mother for advice. Rose Davidman Rodriguez called a family-crisis meeting and consulted her brother, Joe Davidman and his son, Howard. I think, though I am not sure, that it was Howard's idea that Rose should call his sister, Joy, who lived with her husband, Bill, and two small sons hidden away deep in the country at Staatsburg, in Duchess County. Joy immediately acquiesced to the suggestion that Renée and her two little ones should hide out at the farm, and arranged that Bill, who was in New York on business, should pick them up the very next day and, acting as guide and bodyguard, bring them home to the Staatsburg house. Thus the Pierces, mother and children, vanished out of sight and out of ken, into hiding. The Davidman family closed ranks and the escape was complete.

The end of one cycle marks the beginning of another. Tired and frightened, the children bewildered and apprehensive, the trio arrived at Staatsburg, and Mother made them very welcome. Renée shared a bedroom with Mother and the two of them got on very well together.

I remember their arrival. I remember being amazed at this tiny, delicate little person who was Rosemary. Bob was just a boy and I was used to boys. After all, I had a brother, but I confess I was disturbed a little by his neatness and his clean appearance. In retrospect, meeting me must have been quite disturbing for Bob, for I was all angles and rough edges, dirty, scruffy and rough-and-tumble, but we soon became friends and I determined to teach these two strange people the ways of the world, my style. I showed Bob all the interesting things and places and protected both him and Rosemary from David. He was bigger and possessed the enormous natural superiority of a senior brother, but he and I fought with great gusto. Rosemary and I have, to this day, a great affection for each other, though we were out of touch for thirty years and only recently renewed contact.

Soon Renée, Bob and Rosemary were settled in and an accepted part of the Gresham ménage. Mother's much-needed vacation had now become a possibility, for with Renée living in our home, there was someone there to cook and clean and take care of Dad and us two boys. Mother longed to go to England. She wanted to see that land from which stemmed the literature she admired so much and she also wished very much to meet and talk to the British Christian writer with whom she had exchanged letters for two years—C. S. Lewis. And so plans were laid and arrangements made, and Mother left for England for a six-month trip.

August 1952 passed into September and summer faded to fall. Some bright frames remain on the time-bleached mental reel of film from those months; for one, the day when Bob and Rosemary watched aghast as, in fending off an assault by David, I suffered a badly mutilated finger and bled profusely all over the place. I carry that scar today. Bob and Rosemary, who were always (and still are) very close, were often bewildered by the distance between David and me. My seventh birthday stands out alive in my mind.

Dad was an accomplished amateur conjurer or magician and for my birthday party he put on a striking performance, to the delight of all the neighbourhood children and Bob and Rosemary, who, I think, were already beginning to like and admire him. Among his tricks on that occasion was one where a child from the audience is induced to hold a paper cup with the bottom cut out of it securely on his head while Dad carefully pours a jug of milk into it. The audience was then asked to call out the magic words—in this case, "Happy Birthday, Douglas"—and presto, Dad lifted the cup from the child's head and the milk had vanished! Also, Dad performed with the fascinating Chinese linking rings which seem to link and unlink themselves, forming chains and patterns in the hands of the adept. These conjurer's deceptions date back centuries, to ancient Oriental bazaars and further, but by that time, November 1952, a far older and much more significant magic was at work, for as early as August 1952, Dad and Renée had found that they were ideally suited to one another and had fallen deeply in love.

Now this occurrence was, or at least seems to have been, so inevitable that in honesty I must ask myself if in fact Mother saw Renée's arrival in our household as an opportunity not to be missed and left for England, not only aware of the likelihood of their falling in love, but also hoping that they would, thus giving her the chance of escaping from a marriage which was fast disintegrating. However it may have been brought about, whether by accident or by design, the facts are that while Mother was away in England, Dad and Renée became lovers, and eventually Dad wrote to Mother, in or about January 1953, to confess that he found Renée a far more suitable mate than Mother had proved to be. Renée was beautiful and stylish, with a flair for dress and fashion. Mother was careless more often than not with her personal appearance and more concerned with her intellectual abilities and attractions. Mother lived more to write than for anything else and she loathed the boring routine of cleaning the house and doing the laundry. Renée, on the other hand, found a great deal of self-fulfilment in performing all the tasks of a housewife to a standard of unusual excellence. Dad's innate insecurity had long been aggravated by the inescapable fact that Mother was as good a writer as he, and better educated, to boot (in a formal sense), as well as being of higher intelligence. Renée, although highly intelligent, had no desire to be intellectual and had not finished college. Renée, loving, attentive and responding to Dad's affection, was indeed a woman ideally suited to Dad's needs. Mother was absolutely the opposite. I was completely unaware of the developing relationship between Dad and Renée. Probably at that age I was barely even aware of the nature or existence of such relationships. My world was full of its usual activities, added to which was Rosemary, the fragile, frightened little girl whom I could protect from the terrors of the world.

In January of 1953, presumably in reaction to Dad's letter, Mother at last returned from England, and, for a while, we once again all lived together. It became apparent to me that something was seriously wrong among the grownups. The uneasy tensions I had lived with as long as I could remember began to boil over, and there were bitter arguments, tears and rages. Renée was caught in the middle of this holocaust of emotions. The fundamental causes of this outbreak of open hostility between Dad and Mother were two-fold and deep-rooted. The affair between Dad and Renée was the final episode in Dad's long history of infidelity, and, second, Mother had decided that England was the place to live and to raise David and me, an idea with which Dad did not agree at all. I cannot, nor would I wish to, remember all the scenes which were enacted in our family at that time. The result was that Renée left for Florida to find a home. I was with Dad when he took Bob and Rosemary and put them on the plane to fly down and join her. We tucked them into bunks on the plane, and a stewardess gave them each a pill to enable them to sleep. We said good-bye, and as Dad led me off the plane I looked back at Rosemary, again looking lost and frightened, clutching tightly a huge teddy bear as large as she was, the twin of the one that I had. Rosemary survived the trip despite vomiting all the way, but the teddy bear was a write-off. Airline staff, in collusion with Renée, tossed him ignominiously in the garbage. (Mine also came to a bad end. He was left out on the balcony in the rain and all his stuffing came out.)

Sometime later, Dad left also (I presume, to join Renée), and Mother began the job of selling up the Staatsburg home and all its contents. I held large, glaring black-and-white "For Sale" signs against the beautiful, stately maples in front of the house whilst Mother clumsily hammered a nail at each corner, her vision blurred by tears she almost managed to hide. I didn't know why she was upset. I thought putting up signs was great fun! Renée, Bob and Rosemary disappeared from my life for thirty years, and Dad became a distant and vague memory until 1960.

I have never felt any resentment towards either Dad or Mother for what befell them. This seems to surprise some people, but after all, they suffered far more agony from the wreck of their dreams and their marriage than I ever did. Renée and Dad were married in 1954 and lived happily together with Bob and Rosemary until Dad's death in September 1962.

CHAPTER 3

Transition

WE LEFT Staatsburg and I have never been back. Awaiting passage on a ship for England, we lived for a while at New Rochelle. I loved it; I was seven years old and knew nothing of the sea; crabs scuttled away from every footfall and hid under rocks like schoolboys caught in some misdemeanour, but they put on their dignity and gesticulated angrily with their tiny claws if you lifted up their rock, as if that were against the rules. Amongst the mud and rocks there were many forms of living things that I found new and fascinating. I never wanted to catch them, or do anything to them; just to watch them was sufficient. Of all these denizens of the not-so-deep waters of Long Island Sound, the most astonishing to me, then and even now, were those relics of a long-gone prehistoric age, the incredible horse-shoe crabs. New Rochelle was great fun; there were all the sea-things to see, and along the promenade on the edge of the beach there were usually one or two Military Policemen, who were an easy touch for a Coke or an ice cream. Once, a man Mother had become friendly with took us out on the Sound in his little sailing dinghy. We ran aground, and he had to get out and push.

I don't know how long we were in New Rochelle, but we stayed at some kind of boarding-house, where several women shared kitchen facilities. One of these women was an arrogant, domineering person who lorded it over the others and by dint of a cruel and merciless tongue made sure that she got what she wanted when she wanted it, without any regard for the rights or feelings of others. Once, in my presence, she scolded a pretty, inoffensive little person away from the stove so that she herself could use it, and as the poor girl fled from the kitchen in tears, this harridan pursed her meagre lips and, smirking, muttered, "I guess that showed her who's who around here"! The next day, Mother, by either accident or design, was engaged in preparing supper for her sons when once again the time arrived at which this female dictator was accustomed to use the stove. Now that I come to think of it, an unusually large number of the establishment's tenants happened to be present, all with a casual air, chatting or just sitting around. Anyhow, the dowager opened her mouth and, having aimed it squarely at Mother, began to launch a salvo of draconian verbiage, smoking and dripping with vitriolic abuse. Mother let her tirade continue for a few seconds, just long enough for her to get the impression that once again she was to get her own way, and then erupted, quite calmly dissecting the woman's character, upbringing, heredity and appearance with a steady, lava-like flow of beautiful oratory. Imagine, if you can, an elderly and rather pompous flame-throwing dragon suddenly face to face with Mount St. Helens or Krakatoa. The dragon's flame was extinguished and she retired from the field of battle a defeated, chastened and maybe wiser soul. Mother received a quiet ovation from the other ladies present and calmly went on cooking.

This encounter was of deep significance to me, for it gave me the first realisation that my Mother was something more than just a warm, soft, cuddly "Mommy." I became aware that day that there was in the makeup of Mother's character a considerable quantity of high-tensile steel fibre (just how much, I was to learn years later) and I began to feel that with Mother around I need not fear anything.

The Cunard White Star liner *Britannia* was to sail for England out of New York, bound for Liverpool, in the first week of November 1953. A ship, a real ship, to explore, to run around on, and on which to sail out onto the ocean— and there it was, all white and shining at the quayside. It wasn't very big—in fact, there were lots of bigger ships all around in the docks—but this was *my* ship. I was going to England on it, and I did.

I had told a little girl on the school bus back in Staatsburg that she wouldn't be seeing me again because I was going to England. "Aw, you mean *New* England," she scoffed. "No. I don't," I replied. "You mean across the ocean?" she had asked, her eyes huge. Well, there was the ocean and there was I.

The weather was fine when we left New York. I was tucked up in my bunk when the gallant old *Britannia* spun her screws and headed out of the shelter of New York and faced the Atlantic. I was far too excited to have any regrets about leaving home, Dad, America or anything else and also too excited to sleep. Mother came into the cabin later and I seem to remember that she was crying quietly, but I was on the edge of sleep and perhaps I dreamt it. From the very beginning, I was aflame with excited curiosity, and the more I discovered, the more delighted I became. This new-found world, the sea and all that floats upon it, I found fascinating. For that matter, I still do.

I can only surmise what Mother must have gone through in making the decision to leave Dad and take David and me to England. After all, in one's thirties one is no longer young enough to be secure in the infallibility of one's own decision-making, and not yet old enough not to care whether one is right or wrong, but to take action regardless. As a Christian, Mother must have gone through that agony of introspection, the prototype of which took place in Gethsemane. That searching out of real motive against what might appear as rationalisation of her own desires, or self-justification. Was she leaving Dad for good and honest reasons? Did she have the right to deprive her two sons of their father for her own sake, or was it for their sakes? And then, what about Dad himself? Did she have the right to take his sons away from him? What would Jesus have her do? The break from her home, husband, country and all her past, childhood in the Bronx, New York, family and friends must have been a painful and shattering experience for her. What feelings, fears and fledgling hopes pursued one another through Mother's mind as that old ship slid slowly away from the familiar New World to take her, alone save for two small sons, and shielded only by her faith and courage, to the all-but-unknown Old World. It was probably a weird mixture of agony, relief and probably an almost heady sense of freedom. I'm sure she was weeping that night when she tucked me in, but I dismissed it as just "Mommy being silly."

I rocketed around the ship, leaping up and down companionways and corridors. I found my way to the galley and was rewarded with sweet, sticky cakes and Coca-Cola. I wormed my way down to the engine room and was shown the great engines by the chief engineer. I poked my nose into every nook and cranny of the ship that I could find. "Passengers not allowed on the bridge," said a tall officer with lots of gold braid on his cap. He was indicating with one gloved hand a large sign. "Aw, come on. I'm too little to read that," I replied. "And anyway, I don't see any bridge." "Well, then," said the officer with a resigned sigh, "I suppose I'll just have to show it to you," and with that I gained access to the bridge. I must have been a constant source of worry and embarrassment to Mother, for I was into everything, with scant regard for rules or regulations.

Social activities aboard the *Britannia* included several parties of various kinds, and Mother spent some time aboard in the company of a handsome and charming young Sikh, complete with turban and beard, the former an object of fascination to me, for I had never before seen a turban and regarded this man as a fairy-tale character suddenly come to life. A shipboard romance? Perhaps, but I doubt it. Somehow, it would not have been Mother's style. Someone organised a creative-writing contest (Mother won it). And I had my eighth birthday. A howling North Atlantic gale was tossing the ship around with the ferocious frivolity for which such storms are famous, and I was given a little red "Dinky" car. When the ship pointed its bow at the ocean floor, I, crouching at one end of a corridor, would let go of the car and it would hurtle off toward the far end of the corridor. If I had timed it just right, the car would slow down, stop and then begin its return journey as the valiant old vessel righted herself and proceeded to climb up the side of the next huge wave, rolling savagely at the same time, so that my little red car swung from one side of the passage to the other, for all the world as though the driver were severely inebriated. More than one grownup watched that game for a short while and then fled for parts unknown, making strange gulping sounds and holding a hand over his or her mouth. I loved it—the ship, the storm, the sea and the voyage and all the people associated with it. I remember there were several stewardesses who had a sort of ready-room at the end of our passageway. They were Irish, from County Cork, I think. They made fun of my crew-cut and my accent and sat me upon their laps and generally spoiled me. I, in turn, adored them. All too soon, after a mere eight days at sea, we had crossed the Atlantic Ocean; the first great adventure in my life was over. The sparkling sea, heaving and indignant, the wheeling sea-birds with their perpetual mocking cries and the ever present scents of the ship, sea salt, new paint, hot tar, oil and diesel fumes intermingled in a kind of olfactory pot-pourri were to be left behind, stored away in the dark cellars of memory, once in a while to be deliberately recalled, such as now, but more frequently to emerge by themselves suddenly and without warning.

The ship, sluggish, as if tired after her frolic in the ocean and bored with a mere river estuary, slowly pulled into the Mersey and up the river to Liverpool. As we came into that dank, brown-smogged, evil-visaged port, smoke and fumes seemed to rise from every third or fourth building and a chill, thin rain drifted meanly down from a sky the colour of old mud. My brother leaned on the rail of the ship studying with distaste the approaching shoreline. Finally, he spoke. "Mommy," he said with the full conviction of his nine and a half years, "I don't like England." I didn't at that stage think much of the place myself, but I kept my peace for fear of hurting Mother; after all, she had told us over and over again what a beautiful country we were coming to (she was right), what wonderful people we were going to meet (she was right again) and what a happy life we were going to lead (here she was wrong). Then again, no-one should see England for the first time on a bad November day from the deck of a ship pulling into a Liverpool dock.

A train: pulled by a huge black soot-covered monster of a steam engine, roaring its defiance into the night sky; a musty compartment, cold and yet stuffy, with the black rain beating against the windows from the darkness of the wet hostile night, and that smell—it pervaded every British train that I ever set foot in, a barely describable combination of soot, coal smoke, unwashed passengers and the thick, grey water which should have been changed long since, with which the cleaners had mopped the floors of the passenger compartments.

Well do I remember snuggling up to Mother, with a mixture of feelings—fear, sadness for the end of the voyage—and the warm comfort of Mother's arms holding the world away.

London: the Avoca House Hotel, Belsize Park Avenue, Belsize Park, London. We lived in two rooms in a house some distance from the hotel proper. I found out how to be hungry enough to eat mulligatawny soup from a "tin," heated over a gas ring. I met for the first time the English style of bed that was higher than I was. David and I shared the front room of this ground-floor "flat" and Mother lived in the back room, the larger of the two (though both were large), which looked out through French windows onto a dirty back yard or "garden." Whilst David and I slept in the front room, God alone knows what shared Mother's solitude—exhaustion certainly, self-reproach, self-doubt, anxiety, tears and most certainly prayer.

London was grey; it still is grey for me. London! The very name evokes a feeling of greyness. I love London and I loathe London. Some of the happiest days of my life have taken place there. Only once was I in despair in London, and that lasted for only one night, and yet for me, still, London is a cold grey place. We lived for a little more than eighteen months in the uninsulated, criminally under-heated rooms. For me, at eight years old, that was just the way life was. (Strangely, I was to return to just such an environment ten years later, under very different circumstances.) Anyway, there was Hampstead Heath not far away and many things to see and do amongst the greyness of London.

As soon as it could be arranged, Mother took us to Oxford. It was December. We were to meet the man who wrote the Narnia stories, *Out of the Silent Planet* and *Perelandra*, and of whom Mother had talked so much and so often that in my childish mind he had taken on the aspect of a cross between Sir Galahad and Merlin the Wise.

Another of those memorable train journeys.

I'll never forget my first sight of Paddington Station. We came up from the "tube" station into that vast man-made cavern, roofed over with steel and glass, stained brownish grey by the years of steam and smoke. Echoes of barely intelligible cries from officials and hawkers bounced like little lost ghosts amongst the roof trusses, only to be vanquished by the supercilious official voice from the "Tannoy" system, so amplified that it cut like a knife through the seething sounds of men and machines: "The 2.45 for Reading, Oxford and the North is now standing at Platform 8. First-class carriages are at the rear of the train. The 2.45 for Reading, Oxford and the North is now standing at Platform 8. Passengers should proceed to the barrier please. Thengkyu"! A brief silence, and then the hubbub would flow in again to fill the space left by the announcer's voice coming to an end. And the people, all sorts—soldiers travelling here and there, naval men, a rare R.A.F. type (they mostly managed to find an easier means of moving about the country), looking faintly perturbed at having to spend time travelling at ground level with the rest of us hoi-polloi, and multitudes of civilians, all going somewhere or coming from somewhere else. People at Paddington Station were always either sitting resignedly on the sloped S-profile wooden benches, a study in lethargy and boredom, or frantically grabbing up suitcases and parcels and rushing hither and thither in pursuit of their train, their taxi, their friends or their peace of mind. In addition to milling passengers, some lost-looking and bewildered, others bored and with an air of vast experience and of course those who strode purposefully, their heads held high, marching straight-arrow through their fellow-men absolutely sure of exactly where they should be going (and often wrong), there were the full-time residents: porters with baggage trolleys slowly meandering or frantically dashing about, depending on age, enthusiasm and the briskness or otherwise of business; pairs of hugely tall Military Police who patrolled with stately gait, their bright red caps always to be seen towering above the crowd, peaks down over their eyes, forcing their heads erect that they might see where they were going; the old lady with her two shopping bags, rummaging amongst the rubbish bins, scratching occasionally through the layers of verminous ragged clothing that she wore both summer and winter and pushing back the greasy rope-thick strands which served for her hair that she might lean over further into the garbage, to which, I must confess, it seemed that she belonged. There were pretty over-painted young ladies about Paddington, too, and they were a friendly lot, always ready to talk to a lonely little boy, young lad, gawky adolescent, young man. Once, a few years later, one of these wounded butterflies sat down on a bench beside me and said, "Gawd, if I don't git aht o' this gime, Oi'll wear me feet dahn to me ankles, honest." I hadn't the faintest idea what she was talking about, so I simply smiled and offered her an acid drop. "Ta, luv, don't mind if I do," she said, and we sat and chatted companionably for ten minutes or so, till she remarked, "Well, better do a bit, I s'pose. Ta ta, luv," and off she went into the crowd. I thought she was beautiful. I was about twelve at the time.

I remember the three of us walked across the seemingly endless expanse of dirty concrete and asphalt floor, our feet stirring to brief life the scattered used railway tickets which always lay like dead moths' wings all across the station, and on to the ticket offices, faced with wood panelling, at the back of the station. "One and two halves to Oxford, third class," said Mother. (I was always amused by being one of "two halves.") In those days there were still three classes of rail travel, first, second and third. Second class soon vanished, leaving, in a typically British fashion, only first and third. Then off we went to find our way to the right platform, through the gate at which tickets must be "shewn" and then onto the wide double-side platform to await the train. The loud roaring "whaaoomph!" of a steam loco giving vent to its first protesting grunt of steam made me jump halfway out of my skin that day as we waited for our train to arrive and the one at the next platform began to leave. "Whaaoomph!" again and again and again and with a great clanking of couplings and groaning and squeaking, the train began to move. It always amazed me to see the front of the train moving off quite quickly whilst the back of the train was still stationary. Whomp! . . . Whomp! . . . Whomp! . . . went the engine, its grunts coming more closely spaced as it began to pick up speed, until finally they all ran together into a long stuttering roar as the train disappeared out into London and the greyness, leaving behind only the roiling clouds of smoke and steam which had mushroomed up to the roof with the first few agonised roars of the engine, and slowly faded away, adding just one more layer of grime to the station roof. I had been so intent on watching the train departing that I failed to notice the approach behind me of *our* train, which suddenly arrived accompanied by its own cacophonic roar of steel wheels, shrieking brakes, escaping steam and chattering rails. For the second time I jumped and, clapping my hands over my ears in terror, spun round in time to see it slide majestically to a halt, a mere few yards from the buffers at the end of the rails, the engine wheezing and sweating and looking smug, as if to say, "Ha. Ha. Caught you that time, didn't I?"

We boarded the train, and I bounced up and down on the sprung cushions of the seats, marvelling at all the wood panelling, the overhead luggage racks made of netting hung on brass frames, the brass fittings and the wide leather strap which, with its brass grommetted holes, was used to adjust the height of the window. A corridor ran along one side of the train, and one could walk the length of the carriage to a lavatory at each end, or on to other carriages and the dining car. I have no idea what the situation is today, but in 1953 it was often possible to get an excellent meal on one of the longer train journeys. The London and North Eastern Railway (L.N.E.R.) had recently been swallowed up into British Railways, which became British Rail, which became Brit Rail, which will probably become Bri Ra, which will probably eventually vanish altogether, and no doubt only my friend Broke Mountevans and other train fanatics will grieve. However, in 1953 many carriages still bore the insigne L.N.E.R., and I asked Mother what it meant. Railwaymen were proud of their trains in those days and with some reason, but all that faded with the onset of socialised attitudes. We passed through Reading; Mother pointed out the large red brick Huntley & Palmers biscuit factory and was a little disappointed to realise that the famous English brand name as yet meant absolutely nothing to us, though of course it was a household word to every English schoolboy. From the railway line Reading is not an awe-inspiring sight, but then, what town is? Finally to Oxford, and the always repeated but never explained stop and ten-minute wait beside the cemetery before pulling into the station. At least at Oxford the skyline was punctuated here and there with the spires of the various colleges, and those could be just seen through the hazy, wet December air, heavy with incipient fog.

We caught a bus into Oxford and then up to Green Road Roundabout (a traffic circle), going along "the High," over Magdalen Bridge, after passing that College, with its famous tower, and out to Headington, over the cross-roads and onto the roundabout. There we alighted from the bus and walked up Green Road to Kiln Lane and then past the rows of identical semi-detached, working-men's houses and the right-hand turn of Netherwoods Road to dive into the next, almost invisible, right-hand turn-off, the drive of "The Kilns."

CHAPTER 4

Mother

THERE IS little that I need say about Mother in terms of her early life or in terms of any biographical detail. That is well taken care of in Lyle Dorsett's book *And God Came In*, but I should recount a little of what made her such a remarkable person and mother. For example, she had a genuine eidetic memory. She was the only person whom I have ever met who could read the score of a complicated composition for piano and then sit down at the piano and, having laid aside the sheet-music book, play the piece from memory. She had a mostly unhappy childhood. She was a brilliant scholar. To me, well, she was a mother.

At first, she was big and warm and cuddly, someone to run to when I was hurt (or about to be) and someone to show things to even if she only looked at them "out of the corner of her eye," but it was also always Mother who administered discipline. She was quite ready to hand out the "lickings" with a leather belt, the slaps for misdemeanors, and so forth. Once, she locked me into a cupboard, in the dark, but as soon as she realised how terrified I was, she immediately brought me out, cuddled me and dried my tears. It was also Mother who entertained, for the most part; she thought up games to play and invented stories to tell, one of which I will always remember. At the table were just the three of us—David, Mother and myself; it was during that faded time between Mother's return to America and our departure for England. Money was very short, so Mother was preparing a thick soup of lentils, herbs and dried vegetables of various kinds. She had a flair for cooking and could make the most prosaic ingredients into a culinary delight. On this occasion, she obviously felt a need to make the procedure more interesting and told a "soup story" as she prepared the meal.

Alone and lost in fog in the darkening hours just before the pitch black of true nightfall, somewhere amongst the moors and marshes of England, she was (in the story) searching for a path or a road to lead her back to civilisation, safety and warmth. Stumbling among the tussocky, coarse grass and slipping on the mud she became more and more lost and more despairing. At last, off in the distance she saw through the mists a dim, barely perceivable light and immediately turned her steps in that direction. The light seemed to be far further away than she had realised, and she approached it only slowly as she clambered and struggled across the moorland. Finally, she came to the oddest of structures. It was a sort of tepee-like building made of sticks laid upon each other and with a single window, from which shone brightly the light which had guided her there. A little apprehensively, she knocked at the door, and it opened at once to reveal a warm, cosy room, well furnished—all around its walls were bookcases full of books. The door was held open by a kindly and wise-looking man, not handsome exactly, but interesting-looking, who invited her in and told her to warm herself by the lively fire while he prepared something to eat. With that, he grabbed a pot (Mother grabbed a pot) and he put in some water (Mother followed suit). Mother told of each action he made and then followed it herself, keeping our interest and keeping our minds off our hunger. When the action took longer than the description, peeling and chopping some wild onions, for example, Mother told us about the man to fill the gap. He was a shepherd living out in this wild country to find and take care of lost and sick or injured sheep and return them to the flock, and on she went to describe the shepherd and his conversation and his soup. At some stage, I realised that the shepherd must represent the man of whom she had talked so much since her trip to England and asked, "Was that Jack?" "Yes," she answered. "That was Jack." Had Jack in reality cooked a soup it would have been dreadful, but the story was good, and when the soup was served, so was that. Only now, looking back at this episode, do I realise the real nature of that story. The shepherd on the moor finding lost or sick sheep and/or people and returning them to the flock or the path, the wise man adding a little of this and that to his instructional "soup" of conversation. The setting, of course, is straight from Jack's *The Silver Chair*, one of the books in *The Chronicles of Narnia*, with the Marsh Wiggle, Puddleglum and his home. Mother must have seen and read a manuscript copy whilst in England in 1952.

Mother read to us the Narnia stories, among others— the *Oz* books, for instance—and tucked us in at night. For support, in pain, in fear, it was always Mother to whom I would run. For approbation, in pride of achievement, or merely bursting with an exciting story about the size of a snake I had just seen, it was to Mother that I would go. Mother drove away the terror of childhood nightmares with caresses and quiet encouragement (sometimes shaming me out of my fear with gentle ridicule); she provided the warm arms and soft embrace that a child must have. I probably did not suffer as much pain as might be expected upon leaving my father and my home solely because

Mother was with me, and if she was there, nothing could really hurt me.

When Mother punished me, the slap or the whack with the belt were, for me, nothing compared to the mere fact that Mother was angry at me. I achieved a reputation for crying too much too easily over punishment, but it was not the physical pain over which I grieved, but the emotional blow which went with it. I was a baby probably for longer than I should have been. Mother found it too easy, in all likelihood, to baby me, just as I find it too easy to be too demonstrative to my youngest child. I know that Mother loved me with that deep, searing, pain-bringing love that is the eternal bond between mother and child in a normal family environment; that bond which replaces the umbilicus to rejoin mother and child and tie them together forever. We men are compelled by our nature to forge our own links of love with our children—a procedure fraught with dangers as we try to achieve the correct balance between indulgence on the one hand and discipline on the other, our own childhood our only training for paternity. For a woman, the bond is already there and is amazingly strong, though if either mother or child is foolish enough, determined enough or angry enough, it can be broken.

I know that Mother loved me with all the love a mother can have for a child, not from the comfortings, the soothings of hurt feelings and so on, not from the slaps and from the discipline which she administered, but from her lip-biting, white-faced terror when I, childishly careless, did something foolish enough to seriously endanger myself or at least when she thought so. One occasion I recall: I was climbing a tree. Higher and higher I climbed, calling to Mother (who was deep in thought, or engaged in concentration upon some task or other), "Look, Mommy! Look at me. I can climb, Mommy. Look." Finally, when the distance to which my voice had receded rang alarm bells in Mother's mind, she looked up to see her five-year-old a hundred feet or more from the ground, crowing with delight as the wind swayed the tree back and forth. Mother hated heights, but she came up that tree like a cat fleeing a dog. Then, of course, *she* froze, and I had to help her down! The fear she exhibited for me and my safety far outweighed her common sense on that occasion, but impressed me nonetheless.

On another occasion, when I was about nine years old and we were living in London, we went for a walk upon Hampstead Heath, as we frequently did, and I espied, far away and high in the sky, some beautiful kites. Fascinated, I asked if I might go and see if I could get a closer look at them. Mother agreed, albeit reluctantly, and warned me not to be long. Running, slipping, walking and jumping, I launched myself in the direction in which I estimated the people on the bottom end of the strings were to be found. At last I came upon a group of men standing on a hill, all staring into the sky in the same direction; each had a wooden reel strapped to his chest and each gazed out rapturously along a thin line of heavily waxed cord which led off into the dull, wood-ash-coloured sky. There at the end of the cords I saw them, wheeling and floating, splashes of joyous colour, the kites, high up and far away, and stunningly beautiful. Quietly and almost reverently, I crept up to the top of the hill and joined this group of intense men, standing like druids awaiting a glimpse of the sun. After a while, one man turned a brown leathery face towards me and barely had time to say "Allo, young shaver!" out of the side of his mouth before his head snapped back into line with the others as his concentration and his mind rejoined his kite. It was as if whilst their bodies may have been here on earth, their spirits were up there in the sky with their kites and they dared not be distracted for long in case the tenuous mental contact, like the string of the kite, might snap and their souls drift away with the wind. "Wotcher, kid," came from another. Slowly and with care, always positioning myself so that a mere flick of their eyes was all that was necessary to acknowledge my existence, I began (as small boys will) to ask questions. They were, I discovered, members of the North West London Kite Club; they made and designed their own kites, the strings were of silk or cotton, heavily impregnated with beeswax, the reels were "turned up" by two of their members at home using lathes and then sold to the others, who built on the harnesses. One of them was a doctor of medicine, another was a lawyer, but for the most part they were working men. The kites were huge, up to six or seven feet across, and I learnt much, much more, including finally that it was "gettin' too bleedin' dark to fly" and that I had been there for about four or five hours! I hastily thanked them for their time—"S'orright, kid, we *like* talkin' abaht kites"—and fled. I ran and ran all the way back to where I had left David and Mother half a day before. Mother and David had, of course, long since given up waiting for me and after spending an hour or so searching for me and calling my name, they had dejectedly returned home, Mother in a fever of anxiety. I ran home through the chill fog of the London evening, and near nightfall rang the doorbell of Number 14 Belsize Park Avenue. Mother's face when she opened the door was a white mask of fear, which changed to relief and annoyance in the time it took for her to sting my face with a smart slap. "Where on earth have you been?" she said. "I've got the Police out looking for you." I burst into tears, not from the slap, but because of the stark terror, the fear for my safety that I had seen in my Mother's eyes and felt in her heart, and the knowledge that I had caused her to suffer it. In answer, I lied. "I got lost," I said. I've felt guilty about that lie ever since. I can pinpoint this occurrence with reasonable accuracy, for we were to have dinner that night with my grandparents, Joe and Jeannette Davidman, who were visiting London at that time. Mother had to call them on the phone and tell them that I was safe and that we would be along shortly. They were staying at Avoca House itself. Thus it must have been in April 1955, for during their earlier visit, in October 1954, I had been away at school.

The eight-day adventure of voyaging once again across the Atlantic must have been of considerable therapeutic value to Mother. The unreality and timelessness that infects a sea voyage and causes passengers to behave in quite uncharacteristic ways would have come as a balm to Mother's fevered emotions, and given her time to pause, order her thoughts, and settle her mind into place, time to cancel the immediate past and to begin to look toward the future and to plan how best to use the meagre resources at her disposal. Also, it would have provided a time to cast away into the absolving wake of the ship some old ideas and concepts and leave openings for new ones. I think Mother even managed to have some fun on the ship, for after all, once we were on board, there was absolutely nothing that Mother could do about our future until we arrived at the other end of the voyage. Thus, there were eight days of complete freedom from the necessity to do anything. I think she passed some time in mild flirtation and so on, probably as a reaction of release.

Then we had arrived in England, in Liverpool, and Mother had to take hold with both hands and plunge into the battles and hardships of everyday existence. Long gone was the painful Bronx childhood at the hands of foolish parents. Gone also the radical adolescence, the naïve Communism, the dreamlike marriage to Bill Gresham, together with its nightmares. Mother was now a woman with two small sons, alone in London. She collected her thoughts and began to try to find a way to live.

Mother had friends in England, particularly C. S. Lewis and his brother, Major W. H. Lewis, or Jack and Warnie, as she knew them. Jack was helping to pay our rent in London. Jack helped her to find a school for us—through Roger Lancelyn Green, I think; he was a friend and former pupil of Jack's who had attended Dane Court School and whose son Scirard was to be my contemporary there. Jack and Warnie invited Mother to bring her two small boys for a visit to The Kilns in those first few weeks of our life in England. So Mother took us to Oxford, in December 1953. How the memories of her previous visit, merely months before, must have flooded back, the familiar musty train from Paddington—now nervously trying to keep her boys' minds occupied (or was it her own mind she wanted to keep occupied?)—the bus ride from Oxford station out to Green Road, and then the delightful turn from Kiln Lane into the drive of The Kilns and what for her must have been a warm shepherd's hearth against the chill moors of loneliness and fear, The Kilns itself, the back door and the thumb on the doorbell.

CHAPTER 5

Warnie

WARNIE: Major Warren Hamilton Lewis, Royal Army Service Corps, Retired. Now *there* was a man. When Warnie retired from regular service with the R.A.S.C. at the end of 1932, he moved into The Kilns, the home already inhabited by his brother Jack (C. S. Lewis) and Jack's unofficially adopted family, that is to say, Mrs. Janie King Moore and her daughter, Maureen.

Warnie once told me that he found it hard to understand Jack's commitment to "Minto," as they called Mrs. Moore, and he wrote of this difficulty in his diary. She was the mother of Jack's room-mate, "Paddy" Moore, with whom he had been billeted at Keble College just prior to the First World War. Jack and Paddy soon became very close friends, and before being posted overseas, they each promised that should one or the other of them fall beneath the sword of Mars the survivor would do all in his power to care for and protect the family of his dead friend. (Rather a one-sided promise, actually, because Jack had no dependants at all.) Paddy was killed fighting in France, and Jack, true to his word, "adopted" Mrs. Moore and Paddy's sister, Maureen, as his "family." Jack certainly needed a mother substitute, and Warnie understood that. Mrs. Moore had lost her only son and she needed a replacement. Warnie could understand that also. Warnie found Maureen merely an annoying and distracting nuisance. She was about fifteen years old at the time, and Warnie found the chatter and triviality of a schoolgirl a source of considerable irritation and occasional amusement. I think what Warnie found hard to comprehend was that the arrangement continued far past what Warnie considered Jack's duty to his friend and became a cross upon Jack's back, for, with increasing age, Mrs. Moore became less and less rational and more and more insecure; as a result, she became more and more needful of constant, repetitive demonstrations of affection and filial duty on Jack's part, until barely fifteen minutes at a time would pass without some foolish demand interrupting Jack's work. However, Jack had made a commitment, and Warnie accepted it, though inwardly he sometimes seethed.

Warnie loved Jack with a love rare in its total unselfishness. No two brothers could have been closer. For years Warnie devoted his life to Jack and Jack's work. He answered Jack's letters for him and typed manuscripts on an old typewriter which sat on his desk beneath the window of his study, one of the two rooms which Jack and he had built on in the new wing of the house in 1930. Warnie's study was a dim room, the walls lined with laden bookshelves shrouded with dust, the ceiling stained with a mixture of coal and tobacco smoke. Heavy blackout curtains hung from rings above the windows even as late as 1953, when I arrived, and were religiously drawn (presumably from force of habit) to prevent the escape of even the slightest glimmer of light—not that much could ever have groped its way through the density of pipe smoke.

Warnie did not complain openly about the difficulties of sharing a home with Jack's ménage; he merely gritted his teeth and shared Jack's burdens, though it made him furious to have to watch people taking constant advantage of Jack's good nature. Warnie, a gentleman in all the finest senses of the word, was liked throughout the neighbourhood, which, when I arrived, was made up chiefly of the homes of people who worked at the nearby motorcar factories at Cowley. "The Major" was a well known and respected figure; always accorded a civil "Mornin', Major" or "Arternoon, Major" as he passed by on his regular walks down to Magdalen to work, study or read with Jack in his college rooms during term time.

During vacations the two brothers, when they could escape the ever-increasing demands of Mrs. Moore, would take long walking tours together or with friends, and go for country jaunts in Warnie's motorcycle-and-sidecar combination. Mrs. Moore died in 1951 and thereafter Warnie's life became for a while close to idyllic. He and Jack would spend hours together talking or merely sitting in silent companionship, each with a book in hand, the only sound being the occasional lighting of a cigarette or pipe, the scratch of the match, the sputter and hiss of the sulphur flare, and then the often inaccurate casual toss of the match in the vague direction of the fire, which registered its protests by softly clicking and collapsing. At long intervals, one or the other of the two would break the comfortable silence, saying "Your turn, brother"; this without so much as raising his eyes from his book. Then either Jack or Warnie would rise and slowly and easily replenish the supply of coal or wood on the fire, thus rejuvenating it and helping, as Warnie would say, to "get up a good fug," which was how they described the noxious atmosphere in which they were both most happy. Smoke, warmth and silence. Warnie loved to spend a few hours in a completely "fugged-up" room and then grasp his hat and stick and plunge out into the invigorating fresh air.

Warnie did *not* like to have his routines and patterns of

life changed. He was a man whom years in the Army had given a devotion to ordered habits and daily routines; he liked to know what each day would bring as he rose from his bed each morning. His years in the Army had also left him with a dark legacy of alcoholism, a disease which he fought with astonishing valiance for year after year, achieving some successes and suffering some cataclysmic failures. Warnie revelled in the peace and quiet of The Kilns in 1951 after Mrs. Moore died. (Maureen had married in 1940.) Jack, his beloved and respected brother, could finally work uninterrupted and in peace, and Warnie finally took his rightful place in The Kilns household—that of brother, counsellor and friend to Jack. They shared their thoughts, they shared the chores around the house and they shared their friends, their fellowship and good company. Rambling the woods of The Kilns together, wreathed in a cloud of tobacco smoke, walking sticks in hand, they discussed every imaginable topic. They wandered Shotover Hill, cutting down the occasional stinging nettle with a blow from the stick (always the curve-topped ash walking stick of the English countryman). Together, they would stride down to Oxford for Inklings meetings, the walking sticks stabbing the ground behind them in time with the fall of the left heel and with every fourth step swung forward and then back, missing one pace and then meeting the ground again at the following left footfall; sometimes, if the bearer of the stick was in a particularly jovial mood, the stick might even be twirled in a complete rotation before once again falling with the left foot. A man not to the manner born (or at least brought up) looks foolish attempting to use a walking stick, for it always looks like an extra appurtenance with which he does not know quite what to do, but in the hands of one brought up with it, the stick becomes a part of him, expressing his moods and aiding his progress.

Heads held high, the two brothers would follow the paths that they had trodden for years, but now they returned to The Kilns more gladly and with lighter hearts, secure in the knowledge that there would be no trivial but insistent demands made upon their time by Mrs. Moore. Peace, quiet and, most important, solitude; the time to be together and to re-establish the closeness that years of life with Mrs. Moore had broken down, thirty-three years in fact, but now peace and tranquillity had finally arrived for the brothers.

On the 10th of January, 1950, amongst the usual clutter of Jack's morning mail was a letter from a new source, one Mrs. W. L. Gresham, from somewhere near New York. Unremarkable initially, for Jack received letters from all over the world, most of which Warnie would answer for Jack and then take to Jack for his approval and signature. Jack could not type and his handwriting was not exactly the most legible in the world, so Warnie handled the bulk of his correspondence. However, this letter *was* remarkable in its content, for it was written with imagination and style, was both interesting and amusing and was evidence of a lively and intelligent mind. This letter was one that Warnie took to Jack for his personal perusal, and soon Jack and Mrs. Gresham were "pen-friends." Her letters were always welcome, and Jack found that in his replies he could use the full extent of his intellect and his knowledge and neither be misunderstood nor move outside the sphere of knowledge of his correspondent.

Warnie and Jack continued to live in gentle harmony at The Kilns. Warnie's occasional drinking bouts disgusted him as much as they worried Jack, and he tried his level best to conquer this, his one great weakness.

Warnie was deeply interested in seventeenth-century France and became a recognised authority on this era, publishing, in all, seven volumes relating to Louis XIV and his world. He enjoyed his own success no more than he delighted in Jack's. He had no jealousy of Jack's rising renown and he was deeply disappointed when Jack failed to be elected to the Professorship of Poetry in 1951. (The Chair went to C. Day Lewis.)

In 1952, Warnie met Mrs. Gresham for the first time, when she visited Oxford, and after some initial reserve on his part (typical of him) he found her to be likeable, intelligent, conversationally stimulating and amazingly uninhibited. Early in their acquaintance, at a luncheon at Magdalen, she turned to Warnie and said "in the most natural tone in the world," as he recorded in his diary: "Is there anywhere in this Monastic establishment where a lady can relieve herself"? (*Brothers and Friends*, by Clyde Kilby and Marjorie Mead, Harper and Row, 1982.)

Mrs. Gresham and Warnie soon became friends, for she had the rare ability to converse, walk, drink and behave sufficiently as an equal and a colleague to put Warnie completely at his ease, a state which he rarely obtained when in the company of a member of the opposite sex, and this without in any way sacrificing one whit of her femininity. She and Warnie and Jack spent many happy times together during her sojourn in England; walking, talking and enjoying an occasional pub lunch, a pork pie or two and a pint of bitter. When at last she left to return to America, Warnie found that he regretted her departure and hoped that they might meet again.

In 1953, Warnie's first volume on French history, *The Splendid Century*, was submitted and accepted for publication. It had taken him almost eleven years to write.

In 1953 also, Warnie's friend (and Jack's) Mrs. Gresham returned to England after fleeing with her two small sons, David and Douglas, from a collapsed marriage, an impending divorce and a frightening and clouded future, and found accommodation in London. Warnie and Jack were both worried and concerned for their friend and decided to invite her to bring her two boys (already "fans" of Jack's Narnia tales) to Oxford, to pay a four-day visit to The Kilns. At The Kilns the day had been cold, clear and frosty, although Oxford itself lay fog-shrouded, the winter chill of December 1953 firmly imposing its will upon the land. Warnie and Jack sat by the fire in the common room, both awaiting with agreeable anticipation their reunion with their American friend Joy Gresham and, with some trepidation, meeting her two sons, David, aged nine and a half, and Douglas, aged eight.

CHAPTER 6

Jack

LIEUTENANT CLIVE STAPLES LEWIS, 2nd Battalion, Somerset Light Infantry, fought in the First World War, was injured at the Battle of Arras in 1918 and was returned to England.

A misunderstanding typical of the Lewis family developed a rift between him and his father, by which he was deeply wounded; it was simply one of those foolish breakdowns of communication caused by two people using differing idiom. Jack, by this time in his life, thoroughly English in his pattern of thought, had telegraphed his father before departing for the Front in terms which any English parent would have understood immediately to have meant that he was about to leave for the blood-spattered, stinking mud of shell-shattered France, perhaps never to return, and asked that his father come to England to see him off. Albert Lewis, as thoroughly Irish in his thinking as Jack was English, did not, could not or would not understand the telegram and merely wrote back asking for a letter phrased in clearer terms, but by that time Jack was in action. He told me little of his time in the trenches. "Always trust a good Sergeant. He can get you out of more trouble than you can get yourself into," he once said, ruefully shaking his head at some memory or other. Jack had a good Sergeant; a man who confided in him that the most dangerous thing in the Army was a "Lieutenant with a map"; a man who, roaring like an angry bull, led a squad with fixed bayonets into a shattered French farmhouse on the off chance that a few Boche might be hiding there. Jack, sceptical of his Sergeant's caution, waited outside the front door as his men went in the back door. Much to his amazement, about thirty terrified German soldiers poured out of the front door and, practically weeping with fear, ran up to Jack to surrender! They were led by two men who pointed repeatedly at their shoulder badges and said, "Offizier, Offizier." It appeared that they had been told that all prisoners, with the exception of officers, were being shot out of hand by the barbaric British. Jack was not helped in his embarrassment by a mental block which caused him to forget every word of every language he knew, except French! When he finally addressed his prisoners in French, they grew even more frightened; it seemed the French really *were* shooting prisoners. Finally, Jack was able to reassure them and send them off to await a detail of guards at a nearby bridge. The Sergeant, who had by now emerged from the house, remarked that Jack might at least have drawn his pistol! Jack said that it never crossed his mind; everything happened so fast, and with such an air of unreality. That Sergeant was the man who died to save Jack's life.

Jack was wounded by one of those criminal ineptitudes that so characterised that diabolic conflict. An artillery barrage was mounted by an English battery to pin the German troops down in their trenches and protect the British infantry as they advanced on the enemy lines. At the appointed time, Jack led his troops over the top of the parapet and towards the enemy, but as they advanced, the artillery, instead of advancing before them, as was the plan, began to fall shorter and shorter, until "it was falling all amongst us." Jack watched with horror as his men were blown to pieces by their own covering fire, "and then suddenly," as Jack put it, "the ground in front of me seemed to come up very slowly and hit me in the face, and the next thing that I knew was that I was in a field hospital. I owe my life to my Sergeant, poor man. He was between me and the shell and he was blown to bits. I was only hit by the shrapnel that missed him."

Jack was moved back behind the lines and then further back, eventually back to England. For some reason, whilst he was still very ill, the only sustenance which he could tolerate and which was available was champagne. "I lived on champagne for weeks," he said. "I've never liked the stuff since."

Jack was at least out of the War; he convalesced in England and was demobbed at the end of the War without having to return to action. In that same year, 1918, the news came through that Paddy Moore had been killed fighting gallantly with a handful of men against a hugely superior number of enemy troops, Jack, true to his promise, promptly took on the responsibility for Mrs. Moore and her daughter, Maureen. Thereafter, he often referred to Mrs. Moore as his mother and to Maureen as his sister. Maureen regarded both Jack and Warnie as her brothers. Mrs. Moore, as the years passed, became more and more dependent on Jack and increasingly demanding of his time, as I have said. Jack, true to his nature, never complained; he performed endless chores, needless duties and trivial errands, all with good grace and tolerance. His work was interrupted every fifteen minutes or so towards the end. Warnie kept silent, although Jack could see that he was furious. On the one occasion when Warnie decided to broach the subject of why Jack tolerated their increasing burden, Jack made it quite clear that this was one topic that he did not wish to discuss, even with his dear brother. Warnie never raised the matter again.

Eventually, in 1940, Maureen married one Leonard Blake, a music teacher, who was later to become an authority on music education. And then, eleven years later, Mrs. Moore died. Jack expressed no relief at the lifting of this millstone from around his neck, but he became happier and more relaxed than he had been for many a year. He settled gently and comfortably into the pattern of middle-aged bachelordom with Warnie and prepared to live out his life in such style. The Kilns was their haven, and Oxford their comfortable, friendly sea, inhabited by good friends, men of intellect and worthy opponents for lively debate. Jack wore his shabby old clothes and his old fisherman's hat of Irish tweed; he wrote, he read, he taught. Jack was, in a Hobbit-like way, comfortable and at peace. He was an academic success and a literary success. Those things which he could not do for himself, such as keeping up with his ever increasing volume of correspondence, he delegated to Warnie, who gladly acted as his private secretary.

"Mr. Lewis" was a man noted for his generosity. He helped with the education of many children by means of a secret charity fund known as "Agaparg" and personified as an imaginary giant of kindly disposition. This fund had been set up by his lawyer and friend, Owen Barfield. No tramp or beggar would be turned away empty-handed by Jack. Although convinced of his own poverty, he would gladly give to anyone who asked. He had no sense of money management and cared less. He did worry about people, however. He worried during the Second World War whilst Warnie, who had been re-called to active duty, was away, and he worried about the safety not only of his brother, but of the rest of his household as well. He had Fred Paxford, The Kilns gardener/handyman and occasional cook, build a concrete air-raid shelter up by the pond. (It's there to this day.) When a Nazi invasion of England seemed imminent, Jack was convinced that his own life was already forfeit, because he was well aware that the work he had done to encourage Royal Air Force personnel in a series of lectures delivered at bases around the country would not have escaped the enemy's notice. He also considered that anyone found in possession of a firearm would be singled out for special attention (presumably by the S.S.), so in the early dawn-light hours one morning he cast his old Enfield Webley service pistol into the Cherwell from Magdalen Bridge. He told me, years later of course, referring to Mrs. Moore, the servants, and "June," an evacuee who was staying at The Kilns, "I had no right to endanger them further by any foolish and useless gesture. A pistol is not much good, you know, against machine guns."

After Mrs. Moore died, Jack's life had settled for the first time into a calm and relaxed daily routine.

Then began the happy days: days of hilarious, uproarious meetings of the Inklings (friends and fellow writers who read their works in progress aloud to one another), of long walks with friends, and, at home, peace and quiet, the company of Warnie, and time—time in which to work, time in which to write to pen-friends or personal acquaintances. Mrs. Gresham was one of those who fell into the first category, and lively and interesting letters passed between them before her visit in 1952. Jack found her a stimulating companion, one whose mind and knowledge were at least the equal of his own. Warnie liked her, too, and the three of them had many merry meetings. She consulted Jack on her book *Smoke on the Mountain*, which he found cast new light on some aspects of the Ten

Commandments, even for him. He had never looked at them from a Jewish viewpoint before. Mrs. Gresham also consulted both Jack and Warnie on her domestic difficulties at the time. The three became good friends, and it was with regret that they parted when the time came for Joy, as they knew her, to return to America. Jack once again settled back into his usual routines.

During the following year, Joy wrote to Jack and Warnie to tell them that her marriage seemed irretrievable, her husband had physically assaulted her and that she was leaving America with her two sons to come to England to try to rebuild her life. Jack immediately wrote back to promise her any assistance within his power to give which would help her to settle into her new surroundings. In December, after she had managed to find (partly through Jack's indirect help) a place to live in London, he invited her to bring her two sons for that four-day visit.

In some concern over the possible disruption of his orderly household, Jack nonetheless awaited Joy's arrival with the pleasant anticipation of once again seeing a good friend whom he hoped he could comfort and assist in a world which had become suddenly very difficult for her. He sat by the fire in the common room, his attention half on his book and half listening for the doorbell. When the ring came, Jack bounded to his feet and, followed by Warnie, hurried to the back door, hearing Mrs. Miller, the cook, greeting their guests.

CHAPTER 7

Foreshadows

DECEMBER in England is cold, but often cheerful; the weather varies widely across the country and from day to day. The best December weather for me is cold, clear and still. That day in 1953 when we walked up the drive of The Kilns had changed as we made our journey. London had been, as always, grey, with its usual mixture of damp fog and sharp-scented coal-smoke trying hard to obscure the sun, which was doing its best to dispense at least a little good cheer upon the city. Oxford had been clearer and cleaner, but still there was the threat of fog hanging around the rivers and the lowlands surrounding them. However, as we climbed Headington Hill, first the upper deck and then suddenly the whole of the bright red Number 2 bus emerged into clear air, sunshine and the sparkle that cold imparts to the visual clarity of any scene. Clear and bitter cold, sharp and stark, were the weather and the scenery. The trees naked, and wisely unashamed, stood patiently waiting for spring, dozing, it seemed, in the cold, pale sunshine. There were many trees along the drive of The Kilns, a row of stately and beautiful silver birches, which have now long since suffered the fate of royal execution at the hands of those to whom expedience is of more value than beauty. We walked up this drive slowly, for little boys must needs look at things. The drive forked at an old clapboard garage, and we took the left fork, past a battered sign (now in the Wade Center) attached to the left-hand corner of this weathered building, which read THE KILNS, and on between two tall, close-clipped privet hedges. I was wearing one of those typically American long-peaked hats with ear muffs that could be raised or lowered at will, and must have presented to that very English garden at least as strange an aspect as it did to me. I could almost feel the trees raising their eyebrows as I walked past. We approached the house, a charming brick building, by the back way. The house itself appeared not to have actually been designed, but to have just grown, and indeed that is very much what had happened. A brick archway led to a dark green painted door with an old-fashioned thumb-pan latch. Beside the door was a white porcelain button, set in a surround of dull metal and bearing the legend PRESS.

Mother pressed the doorbell button, and almost at once the green door swung inward to reveal an extraordinary figure, a short round lady whose head seemed to be attached directly to her torso in the absence of any form of neck. She was almost bald, and her eyes, small and set fairly carefully, like little jewels, twinkled from about halfway up her face. She was smiling hugely, her thinnish lips expressing both welcome and humour. This was Mrs. Miller, the cook and housekeeper of The Kilns. With much ado, she began to engage in what Jack and Warnie would refer to as "kafuffle," bustling around in small circles and crowing with delight, welcoming Mother with a mixture of respect and familiarity and, to my extreme embarrassment, calling down silent imprecations upon her own head (from me) by remarking upon my intrinsic "sweetness" and visible "cuteness," and all of this in the thirty seconds or so that it took for Mother, pushing us boys ahead of her, to cross the threshold.

The twitter ceased abruptly as a booming voice called out, "Aha! Here they are. Here they are!" and another, only slightly less boisterous, said, "Well, hello, hello, hello," and into my ken stepped two characters as odd to me as any (with the possible exception of Mrs. Miller) that I had seen in all my life. The first voice came from a slightly stooped, round-shouldered, balding gentleman whose full smiling mouth revealed long, prominent teeth, yellowed, like those of some large rodent, by tobacco staining. He was wearing the oddest clothes, too! Baggy grey flannel trousers, dusty with cigarette ash and sagging at the turn-ups (equally full of ash), an old tweed jacket with the elbows worn away, an open soft-collared shirt which had once, in all probability, been white and backless black leather slippers (in fact, they had backs, but over the years they had been trodden flat, for he only ever thrust his feet into them, and never actually put them on). His florid and rather large face was lit as if from within with the warmth of his interest and his welcome. I never knew a man whose face was more expressive of the vitality of his person. This, I was told, was Jack.

I think I hid my face in Mother's skirt, for I was keenly disappointed. Here was a man who was on speaking terms with King Peter, with the Great Lion, Aslan himself. Here was the man who had been to Narnia; surely he should at least wear silver chain mail and be girt about with a jewel-encrusted sword-belt. This was the heroic figure of whom Mother had so often spoken? Well, so much for imagery. Behind Jack came a slightly stouter man, with a full but neat moustache, nicotine-stained; his face was rounder than Jack's, and his smile seemed to encompass his entire visage, not by dimension, but with its warmth. His eyes sparkled with humour and his whole bearing seemed to express his delight at our arrival. Warnie was better dressed than Jack, though in much the same style, softer spoken, though with equal pitch and effect, and possessed as lively a wit and a wider, though less powerful, mind. All this I grasped either instantaneously or over the following twenty years—the realisation probably immediate, the evaluation slowly maturing as my mind developed.

That first visit to Oxford was a great success. Mother enjoyed once again the company of two men whose minds were on a par with her own. I loved the woods and the lake of The Kilns and ran through the wet, muddy fallen leaves, with Jack occasionally booming out "This way, this way" as we traversed Shotover—Mother and Warnie following along at a more sedate pace. We went down to Magdalen and were taken for a walk in the Deer Park. I felt keenly my own self-importance as we strolled nonchalantly through the inquisitive deer (who, very sensibly, kept their distance) and climbed Magdalen Tower. We were able to do these things because we were accompanied by a "Fellow" of the College. Such pursuits were not permitted to "ordinary" people. We ran around Addisons Walk, we laughed and played. I learned to love The Kilns and Oxford all in that one brief visit. Jack and Warnie had put me in the little end room of the house, beyond Warnie's study, the second of the two rooms which they had added after they bought The Kilns. It had been Warnie's bedroom for twenty years, until he moved upstairs into what had been Maureen's room before her marriage. It was a spartan room, furnished with a hard bed in the corner to the left of the door, a chest of drawers against the wall, a wash basin with hot and cold taps, and pictures of steam-ships and railway engines hung upon the walls. One, I remember, was of the engine which pulled the Tal-y-Llyn train, in which Warnie had shares.

Jack and Warnie had forgotten to tell me something about that room, not from lack of solicitude, for they ever made sure that I had a large copper or stoneware hot-water bottle to warm my bed each night, but obviously because after living with it for thirty years or so they took it so much for granted that they never even thought about it, least of all its possible effect on an eight-year-old child. The room was haunted! Haunted by a malevolent, violent, raucous ghost, which manifested its presence in the early pre-dawn darkness of the death-cold winter mornings. This malignant being woke me on my first morning, and on subsequent mornings, at The Kilns by hammering upon the walls of my room with all the ferocity and volume of a team of homicidal maniacs equipped with jack-hammers attempting to destroy the world. Awaking to this cataclysmic clamour, I would hurl myself deep under the bed-clothes, clutching my pillow tightly around my ears in a vain attempt to shut out the noise. I would crouch there in stark terror for what seemed like hours, whilst the horror beat upon the walls trying to get at me. Finally, the crashing row would cease, and slowly, with infinite caution, rather like a wary tortoise, I would creep, shaking with fear, from beneath the rough woollen blankets, sometimes only to be driven once more into my refuge as the presence, perceiving my audacity, renewed its onslaught. Day after day, such was my awakening at The Kilns, each morning bringing its terror, which I felt that I had to endure to earn the joys of the coming day. Ashamed of my fear, I told no-one, and finally I identified my invisible tormentor: air-locks in the iron pipes of the house's plumbing caused the pipes to shudder and vibrate, knocking against the bricks, the walls of the house acting as a huge amplifier. For years I feared that room, for whenever anyone turned on a tap in either the kitchen or the bathroom that insane hammering would commence.

The days of that visit were, however, a delight. Jack's

boisterous good humour, his loud laughter, Warnie's gentle, delighted smiles and Mother's quiet pride in their acceptance of her and her family all live on in one of the warmest, most comfortable rooms of my mind. Often and again over the next eighteen months I would nag Mother about when we could next visit The Kilns, only to be told that we would have to wait to be invited.

As all things must, the visit came to an end and we returned to grey, cold, humourless London and our equally grey and cold two-room flat. Time, as it will, passed, and soon it was time for us to go to school; the spring term of 1954. Dane Court School, Pyrford, Nr. (near) Woking, about twenty miles south-west of London in Surrey, was the boys' preparatory school which had been found for us, and we had gone to Selfridge's to buy the necessary school uniforms. I thought that they were ugly (I still do); Mother thought that they were expensive; Jack paid the bill.

Little need be told of my less than glorious career at Dane Court. It began ignominiously, continued that way, and finished in like manner. Because of my age, on my arrival there as a boarder (eight plus), I was initially placed in the second form; however, the teacher soon realised that I was well behind the other children in that group and sent me off on the endless, to me, walk across the playing fields to the building which housed the first form. As my slow, overweighted feet crushed the newly formed worm casts amongst the grass, I felt that the whole school was witnessing my dejected walk from the elevated second form down the long flat hill to join the "babies" in the first form. In reality, of course, almost no-one at the school even knew that I existed, and certainly no-one watched as I trudged wearily through this misery of my own making. My first experience of the English educational system was a degrading demotion. With two remarkable exceptions, I was to find all my experiences of the English educational system no less degrading, as had both Jack and Warnie before me.

I had never lived away from a "home" of some sort before, and I missed my mother desperately. I spent hours in tears day after day, but I soon found that there were worse things than being away from home—having an American accent was one. I learned quickly to speak like an English child, my training at the fists and boots of my school contemporaries, all bigger than I was. The Masters of such schools will always tell you that such things don't (or didn't) happen; of course, they never happen when the Master is present, but I have seen a boy beaten insensible by laughing children, his only crime possessing an unusual name, and I have been a boy beaten beyond resistance and then hung by his ankles from a tree, with a rope, finally to free himself by exercising exceptional agility and a sharp pocket-knife, only to be punished for arriving late in class. To the Devil with such schools; I hope they all rot from pecuniary debilitation! I was attacked mercilessly for wearing home-made underwear; if I answered back, I was pounded senseless. In defence, I invented grandiose stories about myself to improve my standing in the eyes of my fellow-pupils, a habit that has remained with me ever since (at last I am beginning to conquer it). Condemned through no fault of my own to be different, to stand out from my peers, I decided that I would be at least interestingly different and if possible enviably and admirably different. I became renowned as a story-teller. "Gresham's latest tall story" became a catch-cry at the school. After lights out, it was often I who was asked to tell a story. I mutilated Narnia, *The Lion, the Witch and the Wardrobe* and the others (I hate to think what Jack's reaction would have been to my versions). I soon began, however, to create my own ghost stories, tales of adventure and fascinating scenarii which could be changed at will as soon as someone asked an awkward question. Again and again I would exhaust myself entertaining fellow dormitory members, until, upon pausing in the narrative, I found that they were all asleep. Sometimes, I silently cried myself to sleep.

Slowly, and with great difficulty, I began to fit, never in the mainstream of the school, never in a clique, but at least on the outer periphery of acceptance. Of the teachers, some I liked, some I loathed, most I ignored. Very few bothered or managed to teach me anything. Mr. Hill I liked; Jack met him and Jack liked him, too. He was a Latin Master and, while I never learnt a great deal of Latin, he started an archery club and taught me how to use a longbow and for that I am still in his debt. "Colonel Buckshot" I admired and liked and I could never fool him. "Mitchie," "Moorish Man" and "Mr. Robin" all remain in my mind as men I liked and admired and, now that I think of it, they shared a quality that put them all into a particular category. These men were honest; honest with themselves and with their pupils. Teachers cannot for very long deceive their pupils about the nature of their own personalities, nor should they have to, and if they try, very soon they will find themselves feared, and disliked, or despised and mocked. Of the rest of those who tried to educate me at Dane Court, the ones I remember at all were either figures of fun, tyrants, or ineffectual, but good, men of whom I was often fond and often pitying.

I went there, as I said, when I was just a little over eight years old. I learnt whilst there how to fight savagely and dangerously with no regard for rules or honour and was soon left alone. I left there nearly six years later, the only boy in a dormitory of nine who never shared his bed with one of the others (thank God for odd numbers). When I arrived at the next institution, which was to attempt to instil some learning into my head, it was found that I did not know how to write! In those years I lived at Dane Court, I lived lonely, afraid, frustrated and for much of the time hungry. All in all, it was probably a fairly typical example of a medium- to low-priced "prep" school for boys. For me, it was a waste of my time and Jack's money.

School holidays were a different matter, however. Initially, back to London and Belsize Park. London has delights for a small boy and these I did learn to enjoy; tube-trains, double-deck buses, Madame Tussaud's, Regent's Park Zoo, Primrose Hill and, above all, Hampstead Heath, nearby and accessible. On the Heath amongst the gorse and hawthorn one might find the occasional rabbit, though starving city cats made their lives perilous; and even hints of other more interesting fauna, certainly an occasional hedgehog bulldozing its way through the wet cocksfoot like some strangely mobile irritated cactus. In the early 1950's there were still rumours of both badger and fox, though I never saw either species on the Heath. There was a fair or carnival held each year at Hampstead Heath, and I attended several of these, finding them very similar to the carnivals which I remembered from my years in America. Friends of Mother's tried sometimes to help by entertaining one or the other or both of her children. I remember spending an evening with P. L. Travers, the creator of Mary Poppins; or at least Mother spent the evening with her; I spent it wrestling with Camillus Travers, her son. We visited a lady from South Africa whom I remember as Phyllis Haring and her son, Robin, and a lady whose name I cannot recall but know only as "Mickey" used to take us out for walks to the Heath or wherever. Mickey used to buy us "cough candy," a hard, brittle, boiled-sugar confectionery, powerfully flavoured with anise. I have not tasted it since my childhood, for it seems to have vanished from the world leaving no trace. (I tried last year to find some whilst in England, but I had no success. "Nah, luv, Oi 'ent sin that in a donkey's age" was the typical response to an enquiry.)

I was beginning to enjoy London, but still it was with great delight that I learnt in the summer of 1955 that we were to move to Oxford, or, to be more accurate, to Headington, a township a scant mile from The Kilns and surrounded by fields and woods. I would be able once more to roam at will, enjoying both the delights of the country-side and the advantages of living in town. Best of all, we would have a house of our own, or at least half a house, for it was a small semi-detached residence in what was then the older part of Headington. To save expense, Mother arranged for us to ride to Headington from London in Pickford's removing van, which took all the odds and ends of furniture, bric-a-brac and so on that we had inevitably accumulated during a year and a half in London. The lorry was an old Bedford forward-control pantechnicon and the roar of its underpowered diesel as we laboured up the old A40 highway made any conversational attempt all but hopeless, for to be heard at all one had to bellow at the top of one's voice. Behind the bench-type seating in those old trucks, at about the level of the driver's shoulders, there was a broad shelf on which we sat, together with Sambo the cat. Mother shared the seat with the driver and his "mate." "Oxford and the North," proclaimed the signposts as we drove out of the grey and into the complacent green of England in August; green punctuated by spots of vivid yellow, where an impudent dandelion or celandine made its presence known. The A40 was, in those days, a fairly windy road; it took one first through Gerrards Cross, then

Beaconsfield, on to High Wycombe, then West Wycombe and so finally to Green Road Roundabout, then down London Road to Headington, where one turned right at the cross-roads and there, about fifty yards along on the left, stood Number 10 Old High Street, our new home.

Number 10 Old High Street, Headington, was (and is) an attractive little house, being the right-hand half (when facing the house from the street) of the building which makes up Numbers 8 and 10. Inside, the house consisted of a tiny kitchen, a dining room, a kind of sitting room and a "front room" on the ground floor, and upstairs three bedrooms and a bathroom. The house was spacious and delightful after our London abode and, most important, it had stairs; at last we had a bedroom each, mine barely more than a box, and at last we had a real garden; there were several well-established fruit trees and good, rich soil in which we would grow a wide variety of vegetables, fruits and flowers. I *liked* 10 Old High Street. Mother thought it was expensive, and Jack paid the bill.

Soon, the house underwent that indefinable subtle change which converts a stark mass of bricks and mortar, lathe and plaster, into a home. From somewhere I obtained a budgerigar, complete with cage (Jack named this bird "Papagena"). Sambo settled into his rightful position as head of the house, as cats invariably will, and we began a new chapter. I helped in the garden and played in the nearby park, known as "Bury Knowle." I went fishing in the lake at The Kilns, charged around Shotover and explored Headington, ancient and modern. Number 10 Old High Street became a household full of life-light and laughter. Visitors were frequent. Warnie would often call: "Hello, young feller-me-lad. Y' mother in, hey?" he would say, standing at the front door, his smiles lighting up our tiny front hallway. Jack was always about, his booming laugh echoing through the house. Kay and Austin Farrer, friends of both Jack and Mother, Humphrey Havard and others; they came and talked and laughed and went. For me this was a joy; a park across the road, The Kilns a mere mile away and a heavenly place for a little boy: mud to slide on, trees to climb and to fall out of, a lake to fall into or pull fish out of. The place became "home," really home, in a very short time and as such it was to last only a very short time.

Jack had become an increasingly frequent visitor and was never left out of any social gathering. Once I recall the dining table set carefully for a dinner party; expected were Jack and Kay and Austin Farrer. Before our guests arrived, Sambo the cat ate all the stuffed olives from the bowl in the middle of the table. As time went past, the relationship between Mother and Jack was surely and swiftly changing in its nature. I don't believe that it took Jack long to develop love rather than friendship for Mother, but it may have taken considerably longer for him to come to a conscious identification of his feelings, and then even longer to a conscious admission of them even to himself. As early as 1955, I, a mere child, could see how he brighted in her presence, and how she positively revelled in his proximity.

In 1954, Jack, for a variety of reasons (detailed in biographies of C. S. Lewis), decided to turn his back on the university which had been his home for most of his life, and he accepted a newly created chair at Cambridge. His leaving Oxford was resented by some of his colleagues, but applauded by others. After many years as a Fellow of Magdalen, it would not have been unreasonable for Jack to have expected something more than he received in the way of recognition from Oxford. When Magdalene College, Cambridge, approached him with the offer of a chair created with him in mind, he decided to make the change and became Professor of Medieval and Renaissance English Literature at Magdalene. During the term-time he lived in his rooms at Cambridge and thus it was only at weekends that we saw him back in Oxford. During vacations, he spent as much time with us as he did elsewhere.

In 1956, for reasons as yet unexplained, the British authorities decided not to renew Mother's visa. Perhaps the increasing tension between the English and American governments, which was to culminate with the Suez crisis, may have had something to do with it. We had to leave; we had to go back to America! Mother, naturally enough, was distraught at this news. She had worked so hard and seemingly so successfully at establishing a new life for us here in England and now, at one stroke, bureaucratic officialdom was to destroy everything she had attempted to build. I was appalled at the thought of having to pull up the new tentative roots which I had begun to grow, and leave; leave what had become a secure warm home filled with love and laughter; leave Jack and Warnie, whom I had come to like and admire; leave Headington, Oxford, England, and go back to America. My memories of Staatsburg had faded into patchy mists and only a few bright beauties and flaring terrors remained clear in my mind. My father, despite his occasional letters and presents, was by now a distant and unreal shadow, neither feared nor loved.

Jack did not want us to leave, for he had grown to love Mother deeply and had also, I believe, grown fond of the two small, active satellites who hurtled around her in wildly divergent, though equally eccentric orbits. Jack and Mother decided to marry, quietly and in a civil ceremony at a registry office. Therefore on the 23rd of April, 1956, I became a British Resident. No announcement was made; Warnie was told that the marriage was one of convenience and charity, to allow Mother to escape from the proposed return to America, and that she would continue to live at

10 Old High Street as "Mrs. Gresham." Warnie, however, knew Jack probably better than Jack did, and wise old fox that he was, he began to wonder how long it would be before he would have to move out of The Kilns and make a home for himself elsewhere. Warnie in his deep understanding and consideration had no wish to intrude into what he saw as Jack's "about to become family" situation, and began quietly to make arrangements for a discreet tactical withdrawal. To his surprise, when he broached the subject to Mother and Jack, he discovered that neither of them had ever entertained the idea of his departure, and had no intentions other than that he should remain very much a part of the family and live at The Kilns as he always had. So with some trepidation, it must be admitted, Warnie decided that in all fairness he would have to try out the new regime before making any irrevocable decisions or taking any steps to explore alternatives. Warnie later wrote, "I found all my apprehensions permanently and swiftly dispelled. What Jack's marriage meant to me was that our home was enriched and enlivened." It has become apparent that Warnie loved Mother perhaps almost as much as Jack did.

Much has been written in conjecture about how the marriage of my mother and my stepfather came about and why. Most of the "experts" and academics seem to agree that Jack never contemplated marrying Mother, until 1956, when he apparently made up his mind to do so very quickly. Early in the summer of 1956, whilst Mother lay critically ill in what had been the common room of The Kilns, I, disturbed by Jack's apparent disloyalty to Oxford in favour of Cambridge, and full of schoolboy dedication to the dark blue, plucked up courage to ask Jack why he had changed from one university to the other. His answer was necessarily couched in phraseology suitable to my understanding, but the really significant part of it was this. "It's a much better job, you see, and when a man is considering getting married, and acquiring two children into the bargain, he has to consider things like a better salary with which to support them." The significance of this answer, which I confess I did not find much of an excuse for what I felt was tantamount to treason, though I did not express that feeling, is that Jack had at least considered marriage to Mother as early as 1954. The subsequent secret marriage of convenience in 1956 is made much of as a charitable gesture on Jack's part, but no matter what he may have told his friends and colleagues, either then or later, this "unmarriage" became very quickly a real marriage in both Jack's mind and Mother's and plans were already afoot for a change of domicile long before March of 1956. Jack was not perfect; he did not always practise what he preached, though he came nearer to doing so than anyone else I have ever met. Jack was not immune to the feeling that *his* case was different. Nevertheless, Jack was aware of what was happening between himself and Mother long before it is generally thought to have been so, and also aware of the fact that it could only lead to marriage. The problems of how to accomplish such a thing in the face of embarrassing opposition, not only from the Church, but also from many of his colleagues and "friends," must have given poor Jack considerable food for thought. The opposition has never died, and to this day foolish "churchians" are still trying to "explain" and "justify" what they cannot accept or understand.

The preparations were made for us to move to The Kilns in that summer of 1956, for Jack and Mother wanted to live together, even if Jack's stated position on divorce and remarriage forbade any physical relationship. All that summer holiday, Mother had complained of rheumatism in her left hip, and had experienced extreme pain. I tried to teach her to ride a bicycle so that she wouldn't have to walk so much, but the pain was so severe that she could not even get onto the machine. That summer at Old High Street had a timeless quality about it; long radiant days of fine weather and happiness, but, as all holidays will, this one, too, came to an end and I had to return to Dane Court for the autumn term. Boring foolish days of senseless lessons and punishments, childish pranks and the usual pastimes of a lazy schoolboy waiting for the next holidays.

Towards the end of that term my brother and I received a letter telling us that Mother had fallen and broken her leg and was in hospital, and thus we were to go straight to The Kilns at the end of term, and not to Old High Street. We were to spend the Christmas holidays at The Kilns, staying with Jack and Warnie. I was almost eleven years old, and I looked forward to The Kilns with glee.

CHAPTER 8

The Kilns

AND SO I went, for the first time, "home" to The Kilns. Jack had revelled in Mother's company over the past year and had shown me all the delights and secrets of the woods and the lake; he showed me the air-raid shelter which Paxford had built and introduced me to Paxford himself, to whom, although at first I could barely understand his native Cotswold burr, I took an instant liking. During one of our visits, it was Jack who discovered on a high shelf in the inside larder, a tinned ham which had been sent in a food parcel from America (during the desperate food shortage in England after the War) by an American admirer: one Mrs. Gresham, to be precise. We had it for lunch; it was very good. Jack was waiting for us when we got home. Little time was lost; we merely placed our suitcases in our rooms. I was given the little room off the kitchen. Then we set out on the walk to the hospital.

Jack was quiet and not his usual ebullient self on that walk, perhaps a mile, to the Wingfield Orthopaedic Hospital. How irritating he must have found my excited schoolboy chatter! I was full of The Kilns as home, the beautiful sunshiny day and the self-importance of going to visit my mother "in hospital with a broken leg." Jack was drenched with dread of the task he was facing. He did it, when the time came, far better than his father had done so many years earlier.

I was a blithe, unaffected boy until I passed over the threshold of that hospital portal. As the door sighed sadly closed behind me, something happened which was to me as inexplicable as it was unexpected. I was engulfed in a thickening morass of external emotions. Not mine, but battering at the unprotected core of my identity. The very "me" of me was assaulted by waves of emotions, heavy and oppressive; fears, hopes, agonies and varying shades of despair. I looked about me as if I might see these feelings approaching, and my mind began to grow its own fear. I wanted to turn and run away, out of this miasma of other people's woes and back into the sunshine, but I followed Jack down the gleaming, diseased corridors, each pace seeming to be drawn out slowly, like one of those terrible dreams in which one walks or runs faster and faster but makes no progress at all, and with every step I became irrationally more afraid and more aware that I had left *that* sunshine behind forever.

At last we arrived at the right ward. A nurse greeted Jack softly and looked at me. "Use this room," she said, and showed us into a sort of small waiting room. My back was to a window as I looked at Jack, who stood ill at ease, facing us. I had felt his tension growing all through the passageways of polished tiles and fluorescent lights. "I'm afraid I have bad news for you. You mother's illness is serious, very serious." David grew irritated. "What do you mean?" he snapped. "You don't die from a broken leg." Jack paused a mere instant; pain flitted across his face as he gathered his strength, and he said two soft, small words which smashed into the glassy hospital silence. "It's cancer." My glance went to David; his face went white and he recoiled as if he had been struck. I burst into tears.

Jack tried to be reassuring, pointing out that there was some hope, but I could feel that he did not really believe his own words. I knew that we had been brought to this place to bid Mother good-bye. Then, when I had regained some control, we went in to see Mother. She half sat, half lay, propped on half a dozen pillows; a cage was placed beneath the blankets at the foot of the bed to keep their weight off her feet. Her face was that distinctive greenish-yellowy colour of the terminal cancer patient. There were black smudges around her pain-darkened eyes, and, worst of all to me, strange as it seems, her hair was tied on either side of her head in foolish little bunches with girlish white ribbons. Mother held out her arms to me, and for the first time in my life I was reluctant to go to her; indeed, I only did so to avoid hurting her feelings. I can see no-one else in that room, only this creature that had been my mother; I know that Jack and David were there, but I cannot see them. Mother tried to reassure me with comforting words, but again I saw that she did not believe them herself, and so, nor did I.

This visit to the Wingfield Hospital had two huge effects on my life, apart from the obvious impact created by the situation itself. First, I became aware that I, and, it seemed, I alone, had somehow become sensitive, frighteningly sensitive, to other people's inner feelings. From the moment I set foot in that hospital, I became aware, forcibly, of the storm of emotional currents around me. Ever since that day, the strong emotions of other people reach out to me and infect my feelings. It's like some strange sixth-sense, and is either a curse or a blessing. I have never been able to make up my mind which. When I encounter another person (occasionally, even an animal) who is experiencing a deep and strong emotional stimulus, even if there is no outward evidence of it, I also begin to feel the same way. I think we all have this skill or sense, to some degree, but for some reason it seems to be overdeveloped in my case. I fear that all too often when I have encountered great fear or pain, I have turned and backed away from it rather than share in such sorrows. The second impact made upon me that day was even greater in import and of even more significance. Jack remained at the hospital to be with Mother, and as we set out upon the walk back to The Kilns, David hurried away, for he had to deal with his pain in his own way. I walked slowly away from that hospital, out through the gates and into the street. Strangely, the sun still shone and the trees still swayed gently in the wind, but for me the world was once again grey. My life seemed to me to have come to a sudden full stop. Suddenly, I found myself facing a brand-new experience, that of being alone, utterly and completely alone. There were several years and thousands of miles between my father and me, my brother was as far from me as I was from him and my mother was already, it seemed, in the past. I was alone. I walked slowly back towards The Kilns, the tears of my cloying self-pity occasionally wandering down my cheeks.

I was eleven years old.

The route which led most directly back to The Kilns took me down a narrow alleyway with a high stone wall running alongside it and at the end of this alley was a wrought-iron gate which led into the cemetery of Headington Quarry's Holy Trinity Church. I walked down the footpath, past the stone wall with its bits of broken bottle set in the top, and came to the gate, a child alone, grieving and full of fear and self-pity in a hostile world. I lifted the latch and swung the gate with its so-slight, sighing squeak of weathered hinges and stepped through the wardrobe door into a different world. Every leaf, tree and flower seemed to snap into sharp focus and glow with colour, life and power, as if lit from within, and I was no longer alone. *He* was there. He had been all along, but now He made me know it and know also that He was sharing my grief and understanding my fear. I was given the knowledge as I wandered slowly through the churchyard, gazing about me, that if I felt that I really could not live without my mother, all I had to do was ask that she be spared. I was not, nor had I ever been, a religious child, but He was there and I knew it. I went into the church and, kneeling at the altar rail, did what I had never done before. I prayed, not out loud; silently I begged that my mother be permitted to live. I prayed with every fibre of my being, mind, soul and body. After a short while, only a few seconds perhaps, I knew that my prayer had been granted. I knew that my mother was to be restored to me. I left the church, no longer alone, and comforted, secure in the knowledge that I had been heard, understood and that my request had been granted. I was no longer afraid, no longer grieving. I *knew* that my mother would live. I should have told Jack, perhaps, for he lived in fear and grief. I should have told Warnie, possibly, but I did not know then how much he loved Mother. As it happened, I told no-one. It may well be that that was His intention. I certainly felt that this was just between Him and me, an intensely private thing. I, at any rate, was at peace with the situation.

CHAPTER 9

The Kilns and I and Others

MOTHER AND JACK were married at Mother's hospital bedside by Peter Bide, an act of deep compassion and charity on the part of this good and pious man, for the Bishop of Oxford had refused permission for this marriage on the grounds that Mother was a divorcee and therefore it would be adulterous. Perhaps the Bishop was more concerned with the image of his church and of Jack himself than with the laws of the church, or the truths they were supposed to support. Had he looked a little deeper, he might have seen that Bill Gresham had already been divorced before he married Mother, and thus that marriage was technically invalid, and that Mother was free to marry again under the same laws by which he was denying her this right and rite. I feel sure there were reasons for the Bishop's decision, but they were not good reasons, being "churchian" rather than Christian. Mother and Jack were married before the face of God in the presence of Peter Bide, who performed the ceremony, Mother's nurse and Warnie. Warnie, when recording this occasion in his diary wrote that "to feel pity for anyone so magnificently brave as Joy is almost an insult." And brave she certainly was; the spring-steel fibre in her personality bent further and further time and again, but it never broke! Mother hated the idea of being separated from Jack for any time at all and hated the empty hours between his visits. He spent most of each day with her at the hospital, but they both agreed Mother should be brought home to The Kilns to die—in Jack's home—her husband's home—with him at her side. The "common room" was converted to a hospital-style ward, complete with a system of bells by which Mother would summon a nurse, or later Jack, if she needed help, as she often did. Mother was sent home to die; come home she did, but die she did not. Despite all the practise she had put in at the hospital, she obviously had not got the hang of it. Instead, her health began to improve, at first almost imperceptibly, but soon by leaps and bounds. "Miraculous," said the medical men and, of course, they were right, whether they knew it or not.

There were no frills, no flashes of lightning, crashes of thunder or voices from the sky, no Steven Spielberg effects, just a simple, quiet, stunningly beautiful miracle. A dying woman being torn away from those who loved and needed her was gently restored to them. Remarkably, her condition got better and better, and she and Jack entered a phase of hardly daring to hope. Warnie supported Jack all through this terrible time; he consoled his brother when Jack's sorrow became too much for him, he worked ever harder on Jack's correspondence to try to give Jack more time to be with Mother. When Jack had to be away, Warnie would sit for hours with Mother, talking or reading to her. Whenever a crisis arose, Warnie would always be there, supportive, but never intrusive.

In those first few months of life at The Kilns, when Mother's health was at its lowest ebb, my brother and I found much kindness showered upon us by friends of Jack's and even by complete strangers. We were taken during that first bewildering, terrible Christmas, to parties at the hospitals, one at the Wingfield and one at the Churchill. These parties were for the children who were in hospital themselves, or were the offspring of patients. They were organised by nursing staff, in their own time, of their own initiative and probably at their own expense. I could not join in the fun and games; I was buffeted by emotional impacts from all sides. I stood alone and silent and I watched as children crippled by polio or ravaged by some other destroyer played games and sang songs with bright-faced nurses, whose happy smiles were there merely to hide their inner anguish for these, their charges. The children were happy, laughing gaily and playing joyfully.

Those pretty, active nurses who had arranged these parties were weeping invisibly, deep within the secret places where women keep the strengths that men can never understand. Occasionally, one or another of these girls would come to try to persuade me to join the games and the fun, but I merely shrank deeper into my corner in the shadows, for on her happy face I could see the pain she would not show, and in her smiling eyes I could see the tears she would not shed, and I was afraid.

Also, I felt that had I played and laughed and sang and enjoyed myself, I would somehow be betraying my mother, who, at that very same moment, lay not far away, stunned with pain, learning how to die.

We were taken for holidays; one at Malvern, at the home of Maureen and Leonard Blake. I found and learnt a new land, that of the Malvern hills. I ran up and down them, sometimes falling head-long and, with the agility of youth, rolling in mid-air, that I might land on my feet and continue to fall by rolling through bracken or heather, and trying to avoid the droppings of the sheep which inhabited the area. I walked, climbed, ran and played amongst the hills and played squash with young Richard Blake. It was fun, but I wanted really to be at The Kilns. I knew that our

being there would have made life even more difficult for
Jack and Warnie and I understood why we had been sent
away, mostly for our own good, but still I wanted to be at
The Kilns. Maureen and Leonard did their level best to
help, with kindness and compassion. They took us to see
Her Majesty the Queen perform some ceremony at the
Herefordshire border. I was very impressed, but I wanted to
be home.

Another holiday was arranged at a hotel in Ramsgate,
owned by a family named Berners-Price. The Berners-
Prices had come to know Jack in a strange way. Years
earlier, a certain lady had evolved a clever and simple
means of living very cheaply; she would move into a hotel
somewhere saying that her husband, a rather well-known,
though not too well known, writer, would be arriving to
join her, and that he would (of course) meet all her
expenses. She would then settle down to a few weeks of
leisure and luxury on credit. After a while, the proprietors
of the hotel would be told that the husband had been
delayed by pressure of business or on some other pretext,
and then finally the lady would vanish one night, leaving a
polite note explaining that she had been urgently called
away, and that all her bills should be sent at once to her
"husband." The name she chose to use when she booked
into the Berners-Prices' establishment, as you will already
have guessed, was "Mrs. C. S. Lewis." When Jack received
a collection of bills run up by his "wife," he was both
amused and annoyed. At the same time, he felt distinctly
sorry for the people who had been duped. He informed the
correct branch of the Police, whose reaction was "Oh, Lor',
we know all about 'er, sir; she's always somebody's guest,
Her Majesty's more often than not," and he ensured that
the Berners-Price family suffered no monetary loss. This
began the relationship between Jack and these good peo-

ple. In 1952, incidentally, when Mother was visiting The Kilns, Warnie mischievously brought Jack a letter saying, "You'll want to read this one." Jack looked at the letter and then shouted, "Good Lord, my wife. She's dying. I must go to her at once." Mother, a little surprised, said, "Jack, I didn't know you were married." Jack explained about this confidence trickster and added that the letter was from a women's prison, where she was dying, and asking to see him that she might in person beg his pardon. Jack, being the man that he was, went at once to visit this poor wretch and found that she was far from dying and far from repentant; it was not his pardon she wanted, merely more of his money! For once, I don't think he gave any, although he did afterwards admit that he could not help liking the old reprobate.

Anyway, we went to Ramsgate. Ramsgate is a seaside resort town on the north coast of Pegwell Bay, which is on the eastern tip of that piece of England that juts out into the Channel below the Thames estuary. I enjoyed Ramsgate, for the sea was there (my old friend, from whom I had been parted for too long) and there were some other children there also, two of them in particular I remember. They were teen-aged girls. I fell head over heels in love with both of them and spent hours rescuing them from all kinds of peril deep within my imagination. I longed to be enfolded in their arms, but I was both too old and not old enough, and they were too young; and I wanted to be at home with Mother and Jack and Warnie.

As Mother's physical health improved, the household became less frantic and less fraught and it became feasible for us to spend our holidays there. It was still a strange and unhappy household, darkness shot through with occasional vivid sparks of beauty and joy. There were long sparkling days of laughter. Mother had a succession of private nurses; some I remember well and with great affection. Nurse Hibbert, for example, whom we all liked (and I adored) quickly became a welcome member of the family and a friend of long standing. Another of my favourites was a very pretty young lady called Nurse Porter, who was with us in the summer of 1957. During her off-duty hours, on sunny days, Nurse Porter would take a towel out into the garden and, wearing a bathing suit, she would lie in the sun unaware (perhaps) that I would be carefully concealed amongst the thick branches of a nearby weeping willow watching her with the strangest of inexplicable emotions and longings. I spent hours in that tree. She was my first introduction to physical lust, though she probably never knew it. She and I became good friends. She even had her own car, a beautiful machine called a Mayflower, made by the Standard/Triumph company, and she would occasionally take me out for drives. Once, upon our return from a shopping trip, she let me sit on her lap and steer the car into the garage. I steered it all right, but Nurse Porter was a little slow with the clutch and brake pedals, and we gently bumped the work-bench. This caused a hilarious discussion as to which of us was actually driving at the time; her contention was that the nut that holds the steering wheel is the responsible component, my counter being that I couldn't reach the pedals anyway and so it was her fault. No damage was sustained by either the car or the bench, however, and so we ran laughing up to the house to tell Mother.

Mother got better and better, and The Kilns began to become a real home. Eventually, the last of the nurses departed, for Mother was well enough for Jack and Warnie to look after her and provide for her needs. When I was home from school, the dinner table of The Kilns was the scene of my real education. Jack and Warnie were both brilliant at sustaining a conversation at any one of a dozen different levels and on almost any topic, and I learnt more sitting and conversing over meals than I ever learnt at school. Once, the topic at the table was that of nuclear war, its likelihood and what its results would be. I became so frightened as David gleefully enumerated and described in vivid detail the symptoms of radiation poisoning that I left the table and the dining room, crossed the hall, and went into the common room, where Mother was still, at this stage, ensconced in her hospital bed, and promptly burst into tears. Mother gently and firmly coaxed out of me what had upset me and then pointed out that it was possible to make anything sound scary if one wanted to do so. By way of illustration, she proceeded to recite the multiplication tables in such a spooky voice that soon, shamed out of my fear, I was laughing delightedly.

Strangely, all through those hard, bad, bitter months, it was Mother who comforted us rather than the other way around. She encouraged Jack and teased him out of his sorrow, she delighted Warnie with her wit and conversation, she cuddled me when I needed it and chided me also when that was required. Mother, from her bed of pain and fear in the common room, became the support and the strength of the whole family. Strange as it now seems looking back at it, had it not been for her strength, we all would have broken down. Mother's courage and her indomitable spirit were the bonding agent of the Lewis household.

Whenever Jack was at home at weekends and during the long university holidays, he would spend his days with her, and a strange and terrifyingly beautiful thing began to happen. Jack became a victim of a condition known as osteoporosis, the etiology of which is mostly unknown; his bones began to lose their calcium and become weak and spongy. This disease is incurable, treatable only with increased calcium intake and drugs to try to assist the body to absorb calcium from dietary sources. The condition is non-fatal, but causes extreme agony, and Jack was often in great pain. At the same time, Mother's decalcified cancer-consumed thigh bone, of which only a few shattered fragments remained, began to regenerate, to rebuild itself, to find some source of available calcium and regrow into a healthy femur. Another unusual occurrence was that on one occasion when Mother was in terrible pain, so much that she really felt that she could not stand it any longer, Jack prayed that he might be permitted to bear the burden of this cross and accept the pain while Mother's analgesic drugs had time to take effect. At once, he began to experience indescribable agony in his legs and for a while Mother was relieved of her pain.

As for me, well, I ran in the wood, climbed in the trees, fished in the lake and waited for Mother to recover. I did not have to wait for very long, for by late 1957 Mother began to get out of bed! By January 1958, Mother's cancer was diagnosed as "arrested." She was up and about, going for drives in the country, out to Studley Priory, a country club owned at that time by a man called Bawtry, and walking with the aid of a stick.

As soon as Mother was able to function again as an active and able woman, she looked around her and took stock of the state of repair of her new home. She decided at once that something had to be done. First and foremost, immediate action was necessary to prevent the house itself from falling apart around us. The Kilns had remained completely untouched in terms of even the most basic elementary maintenance for more than thirty years; the walls (where visible at all between the bookshelves) had a weird, strange, scabrous look; the ancient brass light switches frequently flashed blue fire and stung one's fingers like malevolent wasps, as if they were the abode of diminutive but nonetheless evil imps. Jack's and Warnie's shared conviction that cigarette ash was good for carpets ("it keeps out the moths") had, over the years, reduced the floor coverings, such as they were, to an indescribable amorphous mass, beneath which lay rotting boards and leprous, fungus-festooned joists. The roof had tiles missing as a result of winter gales long forgotten and the constant depredations of the boughs of the huge ash tree that stood complacently on the back lawn. Lest you think I exaggerate, let me tell you that early in my stay in my new bedroom (the one off the kitchen), I fell through the floor. A short while later, I was lying on my bed reading a book one wet afternoon and a message suddenly reached into my mind that I should look at the ceiling above me. I did so and, after a second, saw it begin to fall. With the agility born of necessity, I leapt from the bed and was out of the room, despite the obstacle course of discarded clothing and so on upon the floor, before the heavy plaster crashed down, the impact shaking the house! That was the last straw; the house was dying around us. Mother, having just returned from a very similar state, by the grace of God raised from her own death-bed, decided to extend a similar gift to this friendly old home. The house was thenceforth assaulted by teams of builders, roofers, painters, carpenters, plumbers, electricians and Mother's own impeccable taste. What Jack's and Warnie's friends had hitherto referred to as "The Midden" was transformed into a light, airy, comfortable place to live, centrally heated in winter. The kitchen was remodelled and a modern gas stove installed to aid and abet the aged temperamental Aga cooker (a wonderful machine to sit upon on a freezing winter night).

The house repaired, gleaming under new paint and

tastefully curtained and carpeted, the grounds were the object of Mother's next campaign and soon underwent a similar transformation. Paxford was summoned to long conferences with Mother, and soon the garden was producing a wide variety of vegetables; flowers of all shapes and colours leapt from newly designed beds, roses spread their scent upon the soft currents of the summer air and an aura of care and careful planning soon became apparent. The Kilns was, by nature, a potentially beautiful place; tall silver birches lined the drive, privet hedges surrounding the house were trimmed and shaped, trellises for the climbing roses were repaired or rebuilt, and soon visitors began to remark on the changes.

The more Mother achieved, the more she attempted. Once the house and gardens were put into order, she had the decrepit old greenhouse rebuilt and a heating system installed. That done, she metaphorically dusted off her hands and looked around her for some greater challenge. She found one. Mother decided that the time had come to end the constant invasion of The Kilns wooded private park by vandalistic youth from the entire surrounding neighbourhood. These young people had for years filled the wood with raucous shouts, more often than not obscene, cut down some trees and carved graffiti in the bark of others. They habitually threw all kinds of rubbish into the lake, often including each other. They had no scruples about trooping carelessly up the private drive of The Kilns and past the house to get to the wood. On one horrible occasion, a gang of these insensitive louts approached the house, without too much effort at concealing themselves, dropped to the ground and crawled to the window of the common room to peer in at Mother like a row of evil goblins. I fled the room as Mother piteously said "Oh, no!" and Jack and Warnie, both barely articulate with rage at this cruel invasion of privacy, charged out to accost these louts. I found them shamefaced, walking dejectedly down the drive. I had intended to tear them all limb from limb, but there were more than a dozen of them, and my courage failed me. White-faced and miserable, I stood by the garage and looked at them. " 'Ere", one of them said. "Is that lady dyin' in there?" I laughed and said, "No, of course not; she's just not feeling very well," and I walked quickly away behind the old brick kilns, so that they should not see my tears.

Mother, well again, decided that all this was to stop and told Jack that we must put up a fence and a gate. "It's no use, my love," Jack said dolefully. "They'll only cut the wire." "Well, if they cut the wire, I'll buy a shotgun," replied Mother, not without some asperity. We built the fence, they cut the wire and Mother bought a shotgun! It was a little nine-millimetre gun, known as a "garden gun"; it could barely kill a wood pigeon, but it made a very satisfactory bang and issued an impressive cloud of cordite-scented white smoke. It proved an effective first-line deterrent. The bang of the gun and the spatter of lead amongst the leaves of the trees proved to be very disconcerting to amorous couples and trespassers of all kinds. The number of invaders fell dramatically, until only a few of the bolder types still came. Jack did not altogether approve of Mother's methods, but he had to admit that they worked. Walking in the wood one day, Mother cradling the gun under one arm, she and Jack suddenly came face to face with a youth armed with a long-bow and a quiver of target arrows. "What do you think you're doing here?" called out Jack. "This is private property. Please leave at once." "Yer gonna make me?" replied this young man (obviously casting himself in the role of Robin Hood) and, nocking an arrow, he half drew his bow, raising it in threat. Jack immediately stepped in front of Mother to shield her, until he became uncomfortably aware that he was probably in more danger from behind than he was from the bowman. For as he heard the incredibly ominous double click of the breech bolt, he also heard Mother say in tones of chilled steel, "God damn it, Jack, get out of my line of fire!" Jack hurriedly stepped aside, and "Robin Hood" found himself staring down the muzzle of a nine-millimetre cannon, in the steady hands of someone who appeared quite prepared to blow his head off. Sensibly, he fled. I watched all this from the bottom of the rise upon which it took place and learnt a valuable lesson about my mother—she possessed more than one kind of courage, and thank God she was on our side.

The "shotgun" soon became my charge and I graduated to a .410 and then to a twelve-bore, starting a habit of collecting firearms which has lasted to this day. The trespassers also were my job and they became less and less frequent as I loosed off shots, inexpertly aimed at wood pigeons. Once or twice, I had a little trouble. Once a young couple lay in the grass, an expensive transistor radio blaring from the branch of a tree above them, Cliff Richard singing "The Young Ones," courtesy of Radio Luxembourg. "Excuse me," I interrupted, "but this is private property and you should not be here." The young man turned from his concentrated efforts to smother the young girl, and with an air of extreme menace, said "—— off, kid, or I'll push your —— face in." By the time the echoes had died away and the smoke had cleared, both he and his girlfriend had hurdled the fence a good twenty yards away and were running down the path beside the wood, he leading by yards, as pieces of transistor radio still pattered gently down through the glowing green sycamore leaves. A short-barrelled Bernadelli twelve-bore makes a very loud noise and Number 6 shot tends to do electronic components "a whole lot of no good," as we say in Tasmania. Most of my ammunition was spent in more profitable pursuits, however; the odd pigeon or two, a rabbit now and then and, once in a while, perhaps a pheasant, which would have to be an anonymous gift via Fred Paxford (our wood did not have any pheasantry, but there was a large estate not far away that did). I remember the first time a game pie was served, large enough to provide dinner for the whole family and the result of my slowly growing skill with a gun. I was as proud as a peacock.

The trespassers disappeared, and the lake and the wood became once again the private preserve of the inhabitants of The Kilns, and Jack, Warnie and Mother began to enjoy their privacy and peace and quiet. One side effect of this victory was that for me the woods became a place of solitude; solitude which was, with time, to grow into loneliness.

CHAPTER 10

❧

Evening Sunlight

As MOTHER became more and more a healthy, active woman, she became also more and more a wife. Now The Kilns became a happy home, filled with the riches of life. Happiness, harmony, laughter, fascinating conversation and that holy peace which at times the angels drop upon us to provide a pause in which we may rest our striving minds and bodies.

Mother had reorganised The Kilns, house, garden and grounds; she had even spruced Jack up a bit, bought him a new hat (I appropriated his old one and wore it often), some shirts and jackets and trousers and, whilst he was never elegant and still looked like an elderly farmer, at least he looked like a married one. She also took over his financial affairs and put to rights the appalling shambles she had found there. Jack had no financial acumen at all; in fact, it was one of his small vanities that he was proud of being "no good at all that sort of thing." Mother, on the other hand, had become, over the years, adept at stretching a pound and at managing money. Eventually, she was able to convince Jack and even Warnie that the household was not on the brink of bankruptcy, a belief and fear that had lurked at the back of their minds for years.

Guests began to come ever more frequently to The Kilns and discussion at our dinner table was full of life, jollity, fierce debate and profound philosophy. Under Mother's tutelage, Mrs. Miller's basic English cooking developed into a widening knowledge of the Art of Cuisine, and whilst previously guests had wondered whether the food at The Kilns was safe to eat, they now began to know that the rich aromas drifting from the kitchen as they sipped their sherry in the common room were harbingers of delights to come. A delicious meal wheeled in on a trolley (usually by me) would be laid out on cork place mats with pictures of coaches and horses on them (done in that ridiculous Regency style that made the horses look stretched) upon a large oak table (now in the Wade Center) covered by an intricately crocheted lace tablecloth. The tablecloth was Mother's creation; I had polished the silver tableware and set the table. The dining room would be glittering silver amongst warm, harmonising colours, and filled with the scents of fine soups, rich and flavourous meats and delicious desserts. As we stood behind our chairs around the table and waited for Warnie to say grace (always the same simple "For what we are about to receive, may the Lord make us truly thankful. Amen"), I could, during this short pause, sneak a quick look around the table at the guests and sometimes I saw an interesting look of surprised delight on the faces of those who had visited Jack in the days before The Kilns' renaissance. I saw, on more than one occasion, Mother cast a glance at Jack as if to say "There! You see!" and Jack's returned look of pride and love. Mother, in the early days, spent hours sitting in a wheeled chair in the garden, knitting, crocheting (and reading simultaneously) with Jack at her side, also reading. For Mother then, simply to enjoy the fragrance of the flowers, the incomparable music of the bird song as each species competed with every other to sing more sweetly, merely to be alive, to be able to see, hear, smell, to move and to think were, for each and every minute, a joy and gifts from God. Greater gifts followed—to walk in the wood with Jack, to dig little drainage channels down from the giant horsetail marsh and call them the "Anduin" and the "Baranduin" after the river in Tolkien's *Lord of the Rings*, to talk with friends and share the loving company of such people as Kay and Austin Farrer, and then, at the close of the day, to retire together to Mother's bed. Often and again, I would be up and about after Mother and Jack had gone to Mother's room and often I would go to them to take them a cup of tea, or to ask if there was anything they required. I soon learnt to knock first, and wait for the call of "Come in, Doug" before I opened the door.

I never exactly resented the closeness of Mother and Jack's relationship, but as I would leave them together and depart to my own part of the house, I felt always a little pang of sadness. I now know that what I was experiencing is directly similar to the emotion of a new father as he looks down upon his young wife and his newly born son and realises that he is no longer the centre of her world; realises that the focus of her being is no longer on him, but has moved to the baby, and that mother and child now have a special relationship of which he can never be a part, but which he must learn to support. I could see that Jack and Mother had something very special and very beautiful in which I was not included and I had to learn to stand a little to one side. I felt no anger at this shutting out, for I knew well that it was not in any sense deliberate, or even conscious, but I did feel a soft sadness, underlaid with the faint hope that someday I might find such a love myself. Jack and Mother simply belonged together, and once I had bade them good night, there was no place for me in their room, or their world, for this was their time of solitude and solace, the time when they could be together without interruption or disturbance; my place was elsewhere.

Mother became more adventurous as she began to be happier with the state of her home and she began to look further afield. Jack hired a car for trips out into the Oxfordshire countryside and to such haunts as the Trout Inn at Godstowe and Studley Priory at Horton-cum-Studley. It was on one of these visits to the Priory that a meeting took place that was to have a remarkable impact on Mother's life and an even greater one on mine. Mother was at the Priory one day when a lady walking carefully and painfully with the aid of a sturdy "shooting stick" came into the bar. Mother, of course, also walked with the aid of a stick. Soon, Mother was introduced to Jean Wakeman. Jean was a motoring journalist who had worked her way up to the top of that tough profession by sheer determination, talent, hard work and courage, at the same time battling the pain of her disability. Mother told me that Jean had been lame all her life as a result of injuries she had sustained at the time of her birth at the hands of an inept obstetrician. I was surprised at the anger which Mother displayed in the telling of this fact; she was incensed that such a thing should have happened to Jean!

Jean was (and is) a highly intelligent and articulate woman of great personal integrity and compassion and she shared with Mother two important personality traits— courage and a vibrant super-alive and sometimes slightly mischievous sense of humour. Added to their shared physical similarity in their knowledge of frequent pain, their solid Christian faith and their mutual enjoyment of each other's company was a further bond. Both Jean and Mother loved England and the English countryside, and they were to spend many happy hours together exploring it and (if I know Jean) getting thoroughly lost for the pure enjoyment of so doing. A large part of Jean's job was the road-testing of, and reporting on new models of motor-car as they were released onto the market, and thus she was able to help Mother with one of her hardest trials. When Jack, David and I were away at college and school, The Kilns, despite Warnie's kindly presence, must have seemed a lonely place, and the disease of loneliness would have been hard for Mother to bear on top of her other troubles. Jean rescued her, taking her on long trips around the country. Mother would contribute her comments on the car from a passenger's viewpoint and also her conversation and companionship. Jean would drive and her knowledge of England and its inns was a source of great pleasure to Mother, and she admired Jean for it. Mother looked forward to her trips with Jean with great delight and would pore over maps and tell us excitedly of the places they were going to see, filling me, at least, with envy, for I had to return to school and would not be part of these adventures. Mother and Jean became true friends and mutual confidantes. Mother told Jean of things which she would share with no-one else and, though they did not always agree upon matters of religion, politics or taste, they could argue for hours and finally simply agree to disagree, without the dissent having the slightest adverse effect on their friendship.

I did not miss all the adventures that Jean organised. On one occasion, Jean and Mother decided to take David and me for a holiday; Jean knew of a small and (then) still unspoilt fishing village in Pembrokeshire called Solva. The very ghost of my boyhood wheels over that little hamlet with the crying gulls. I was there but a few months ago and was driven away by my own shadows. We drove down to Solva and stayed in an ancient hostelry called the Ship Inn, a pub haunted by the local lobster-men, whose voices filled the night as they sang their songs of the glories of Wales. Jean and Mother both loved the place and so did I. Ambitious as the trip itself might have been for two ladies, even this was not sufficient challenge for Jean and Mother, and a trip by lobster boat to Skomer, a jewel-like isle in St. Bride's Bay, was organised, the boats captained by Dai Phillips and Edwell Chapman. This jaunt was not without its perils. The stone-built, salt-smelling, seaweed-covered ramp leading down to the boats was slippery and difficult even for nimble boys. For Mother and Jean, it was positively dangerous. I saw looks of concern and sympathy on the faces of the onlooking fishermen, and I was embarrassed as these two indomitable ladies picked their way down, choosing with care each spot upon which to set foot, ensuring that it was free of that pernicious green slime which grows upon stone at the edge of the sea and slides beneath the feet, usually with no worse damage than injured dignity; but of course in the case of Mother or Jean, a fall could be disastrous. The careful, studied placing of the walking stick and their intense concentration as they made their way down to the water level (it was about half-tide on the rise) caused the warm-hearted Welsh onlookers to almost hold their breath, and when they finally made it, everyone began to smile.

Mother and Jean, however, looked at each other in dismay, for how were they ever to manage to get from the ramp to the boat? It was rising and falling with the mockery of Poseidon poking fun at all their efforts. My child's embarrassment deepened. Edwell Chapman also saw their dilemma. Mother, with a wry smile, said, "Well, Jean, now what do we do?" Characteristically, Jean, for whom no problem is insurmountable, was frowning with concentration and determination as she began to work out a plan of action. With a wide grin on his face, Chapman called out from the boat, "Don't worry now," and as he pulled his waist-high sea boots all the way up, he continued, "It's easy, look you!" And with that he leapt gaily into the brine, took three swift strides to the ramp through the surging bladder-wrack, picked Jean up in his arms, swept her gently up in the air and deposited her quickly and carefully in the boat. Then it was Mother's turn. The smiles returned to the faces of the fishermen and Edwell earned a round of scattered applause for his gallantry. Then off we went across the sea, the water sparkling with the ever moving scattered jewels of reflected sunlight, salt spray tingling our faces and flavouring our lips, the quiet but insistent voice of the sea always in our ears, whispering "I am here."

Skomer is a lovely island; it rises sheer from the sea, the cliffs making it difficult of access, but there is a landing place and to this the two men steered their lobster boats to deposit the passengers. The tourists would explore the island whilst the two boats went to retrieve their lobster-pots and extricate their catch. We landed, again with the help of Edwell Chapman and Dai Phillips. I ran off to discover the island's secrets; I met the "Skomer horse." Years before, this valiant animal had plunged into the sea from the mainland and had made the eleven-mile swim to Skomer. Why, no-one knew, and no-one could work out how to take him off the island once he had got there and had somehow made his way ashore. So there he lived, his only company the few sheep and the native rabbits and birds of the island, his shelter the semi-ruined buildings of an abandoned farm, which had long ago worked the land of Skomer. He was a friendly old fellow and I shared my picnic sandwiches with him; aged then, he is doubtless no more than a memory now.

That holiday in Solva was heaven for me. There were

rocks to climb, sharp headlands to clamber around, "the rules" forbidding any contact with the grass at the top, even where it was possible, and, with only the sea at the bottom of the cliffs, every handhold was vital, every foothold slippery; failure to cling to the rock would mean a plunge to the icy water beneath and the distinct possibility of drowning. There were hills covered with heather, bracken and gorse to run up and down. The smell of bees always takes me back to the hills of Wales. The sea was all around me, the rank seeweed popped as you trod on it and gave off the odour of iodine and salt.

Mother and Jean also enjoyed their stay and whilst they motored around South Wales, I went out with the lobstermen and learnt how to handle lobsters and crabs without losing fingers to their powerful claws. I learnt to bait the pots with reeking salted gurnards cut in half, one half on each side of the basket neck of the pot, the quick-tie knot to secure the bait. I learnt how to stack the pots in sequence and to stay away from bights in the line as the pots splashed overboard back to the deeps, for a loop of rope around an ankle would likely take you to Davey Jones as fast as the pots sank and then you would feed the lobsters rather than the other way around. Once in a while, a pot would come up completely covered with brittle stars, an amazingly fragile form of starfish which Edwell called "sea lice." They fell apart if you touched them; they were rough to touch, feeling as if they were made of coral, but oh, so fragile. Once, a dogfish came up with a pot and was cast back into the sea; on another occasion, whilst Edwell was working the capstan winch and I was seizing the pots and helping to heave them inboard, I saw a huge, writhing sinuous mass emerging from the neck of a pot. "Mr. Chapman," I called, "something funny in this one!" Edwell cleated off the line and came to look. Suddenly, with one swift sweep of his brawny arm, I was tossed up onto the cabin roof. "You stay up there, boyo; this one's dangerous, look you." Edwell heaved the pot aboard and, seizing the bait knife with which I had recently been bisecting salted gurnards, he made a determined and energetic attack on a conger eel that was longer than he was. After an exceptionally active few minutes, the battle was over and Edwell had despatched this beautifully ugly creature. Then he showed me its teeth; they were as long as my fingers and as sharp as needles.

Soon enough, all too soon for me, our holiday was over and we left Solva. I returned time after time (the last, with all my family about me). Holidays for all of us, in many senses. Jack and Warnie had for a time a warm home full of companionship, laughter, love and joy—and Joy. Her feminine touch filled the house, in all but one room. Warnie's bachelor bedroom with its spartan furnishings remained untouched. A bed, beside it a little table with a lamp on it (and every evening a glass of milk and a Thermos of tea), a wardrobe for his clothes, one which had come from "Little Lea," their Irish home, a small chest of drawers and a table beneath the window. On the floor was an old worn carpet. That was all, except a stale, musty smell of old dust and memories.

CHAPTER 11

❧

Fred Paxford

THROUGHOUT all the years I spent at The Kilns, I was helped and supported, consoled and instructed by not only Jack, Warnie and Mother, but as much, if not even more, by Fred Paxford.

I knew Mr. and Mrs. Miller almost all my childhood; they were always "Mr. and Mrs. Miller" to me, to Mother and to Jack, and until the last years, when he saw through a fog of grief, alcohol and pain, to Warnie; despite their self-insinuation in his declining days, I never heard Warnie use their first names aloud in my presence. Mother, Jack and Warnie always referred to The Kilns gardener, handyman and occasional cook as "Paxford"; so did Mr. and Mrs. Miller, but to me, he soon became "Fred," and I was the only member of the household upon whom this honour was conferred. Fred would have been embarrassed had Jack, Warnie or Mother so addressed him; he would have felt slighted had the Millers done so. But Fred Paxford and I were friends—not associates, but friends. Our relationship was one which grew over several years. Fred was a countryman through and through; he knew the ways of the animals and plants and he knew the ways of little boys. He was a confirmed bachelor, but, whilst he had never married, I gained the distinct impression that he was not unacquainted with the ways of women. Fred cleaned and mended my bicycle when I was away at school, he built the stable in one half of the pergola which housed our pony, "Cobber." He let me help him in the "gyaarden," as he called it, and with endless patience taught me the rudiments of the art of mechanical repairs, and in Fred's hands it was indeed an art, for who else could have shimmed the automatic clutch of a mo-ped with "fag" paper? Fred helped me to learn of the gentle kindliness which many country folk possess beneath an outwardly hard shell. He and I ploughed the garden with a single-furrow mouldboard plough drawn by Cobber. We took turns, one leading the pony, the other guiding the plough. Fred laughed loud and long (at least figuratively speaking, for in his case a loud, long laugh was one guffaw followed by a series of short hissing sounds, as he laughed silently around the butt of his roll-yer-own fag, which resided more or less permanently at the side of his mouth) when the plough struck a stone and the handle bounded and thumped me in the short ribs, knocking the wind out of me. He left the pony's head and held my head down, bending me double to enable me to catch my breath. "Ah! ss ss ss. That'll teach yer ter moind wot yer abaht, ss ss ss." I had my revenge; I was leading Cobber when we ploughed the furrow that was to end at the gooseberry bushes and I led her so close to them that to save their roots from the share, Fred was forced to lean the handles far to the right, and was dragged right through the spikey bushes. He joined me in my laughter as he pulled out the thorns. Fred and I were friends.

Fred had one strange and wonderful habit. He would, as he went about his work, sing, or, rather, bellow, a wide variety of songs in a loud, tuneless voice, or at least he would sing parts of songs. One would hear the first line of a song perhaps, or part thereof, and then a very long silence, broken only by the snick-clack of his hedging shears or whatever, as he continued this song in his head, and then suddenly he would roar out a few words of wherever he had reached in the song. "Oh, Molly, this London's a wonderful . . ." long pause, snick-clack! snick-clack! "And boi noight they . . ." snick-clack! . . . "pertaters er bairley er wheat" snick-clack! snick-clack! snick-clock! (Sotto voce) "Bugger it!" Then bellowing again. "Fer gold all the day in the street, doo doo doo doo!" Shweet! Shweet! Shweet! as he "sharped" the shears. The worst part about this was that he did not stick to the time of the tune or the same key, and thus it was impossible to judge just when, or at what pitch, the next phrase would suddenly crash out. Warnie never learnt to divorce his mind from the songs, and Fred almost drove him to distraction, mutilating tunes which Warnie had known in his youth. Jack and Mother, on the other hand, found it highly amusing. I learnt many a song from Fred by simply trying in my head to fill in the gaps. On Sundays he sang (or at least partly sang) only hymns and towards the end of October he drifted, together with the rest of Christendom, into parts of carols, and parts of popular Christmas songs. Fred was fond of the family pets and to me it never even seemed slightly incongruous to hear something like "Oi'm dreamin' of a . . . you crafty ole bugger [this to the cat] Christmas just loike doo doo doo."

Fred was the ever cheerful eternal pessimist. The character of Puddleglum in *The Silver Chair* (Book 4 in *The Chronicles of Narnia*) is modeled directly upon Fred. "Good morning, Fred," I might say. "Ah, looks loike rain afore lunch though, if'n it doan't snow . . . or 'ail that is" might well be his reply. Like many gardeners I have encountered, he was intensely proud of producing row upon row of "vegables" and watching them develop and reach a state of absolute perfection, but he had a horror of actually picking them and only did so with great reluctance when there was no alternative. Even then, he would leave it until the very last second. I remember once on a cold Sunday evening (Fred did the cooking on the weekends) he asked me from his chair by the kitchen table, where he was reading the paper, "Is that there water aboilin' yet, young Doug?" I peered into the steaming pot on the Aga. "Just about, Fred," I replied. "Ah! Well, better go an' get the cauli' then, Oi s'pose," said Fred and, putting on his raincoat, he slowly took up a knife and sauntered out into the gyaarden to pick a cauliflower. On reaching the bed of these elegant brassicas, he reached into his pocket and took out his tin of pre-rolled smokes, selected one and lit it with his worn old "Tommy" lighter, all the while ruminatively studying the cauliflowers by the light of his battered electric torch. At last, the fag well lit, he trudged over to a particular plant, unhurriedly severed its stalk, pulled up the root and laid it neatly on the ground. Then, carrying the head in one massive hand, he ambled back to the house, in the back door and over to the sink. He washed both the cauli and the knife and then shuffled over to the pot of boiling water and slowly and deliberately cut the cauli into it. Finally, he removed and hung up his raincoat. I don't think I ever saw Fred hurry to do anything; he seemed firmly convinced that any task would wait for him until he could get to it. Mother might approach Fred; "Paxford," she would say, "aren't those kohl-rabi about ready to pick?" "Lor' luv you, no, ma'am; they woant be fit for a week yet," and then, on being asked the same question a week later: "Ah! They be all gorn ter seed, ma'am." Mother soon learnt to simply tell Fred to pick vegetables when she knew them to be ripe.

Fred was a great man, a man of bottomless compassion and warm humour. His coarse blunt fingers could perform delicate work with minuscule nuts·and bolts that would have me in tears of frustration. It was Fred who taught me to shoot a gun, and many other skills besides. Fred had a twelve-bore of his own, an ancient double-barrelled hammer gun, only one barrel of which could be cocked at a time, for upon firing it, the shock would release the second hammer if it was cocked, so worn was the mechanism. The breech of the old piece was held together with a thick piece of cord, which made re-loading a slow process. I seldom saw Fred use his gun, but I *never* saw him miss with it. When I bought, second-hand, my short Bernadelli single, it was to Fred that I showed it first. "Well 'er feels roight enough, bit loight moind, an' 'er looks roight enough; let's get some cyaartridges" was his reaction. After two shots: "Ah, 'er'll do, Doug; she's a roight sweet little gun." I could have burst with pride.

Fred Paxford was a great man. He retired to the village of Churchill when Jack died, and I visited him there in 1973. Someone had told him that I was coming and, living though he was in abject poverty, he'd laid in a bottle of gin and a supply of pre-rolled fags. He poured me a huge tumblerful of gin and watched over me to make sure I drank it as we talked and smoked together for an hour or so and then, with his arm across my shoulders, we walked unsteadily out to inspect his patch of gyaarden. It was neat and weedless. He had "caulis, taters, roobub, purple sproutin" (broccoli) and a variety of other plants. I left him, finally, waving from his cottage door, and returned to London and then Australia. I went to visit him again in 1982, but his neighbours told me that he had died suddenly and instantly while watching television almost two years before. No-one had told me; no-one knew.

Fred Paxford was one of the finest, kindest and most Christian men I ever knew. He was my friend. He is gone and I miss him. I could never have told him so, but I loved him deeply. I wish he could have known my sons, and they him. I think they would have liked each other.

CHAPTER 12

Sunset Joy

MOTHER AND JACK, in the years between her initial recovery and the later reappearance of her sickness, found such beauty in their love for one another and their life together that outside intrusions were hard put to affect them within the sheltered, glowing cave of their love. When Warnie slipped occasionally from his narrow and difficult path of teetotalism and tumbled headlong into drunkenness, Mother and Jack together would try gently to lift him back to sobriety.

Once I saw Warnie, a foolish grin on his face, sitting in an armchair in the common room, dressed in pyjamas and an ancient woollen dressing gown of a rich maroon colour, his feet encased in woollen slippers. At his side was a crate of Gordon's London Dry Gin. Empties lay around his feet. As I watched, he reached fumbling to the crate and extracted a fresh full bottle; his thick fingers had no trouble releasing the unusual wire latch-top which was used at that time to fasten the caps on this brand, and he raised the dark green glass to his lips and drank—and drank—and drank. At last, he let the bottle fall from his hand to the floor, empty. I thought that to consume a powerful spirit in such quantity must prove fatal. There was a doctor present at the time—I don't know who, but it was not Humphrey Havard, our usual family doctor. I asked this man how it could be possible for Warnie to consume so much alcohol and yet live. He postulated that perhaps there was so much of the poison in Warnie's system already, that he simply could not absorb any more and that any further booze he drank would simply pass straight through. I discovered another reason a few days later, when Warnie was safely in hospital.

Coming in from the garden, hot and thirsty, I swept into the inner larder, for Mrs. Miller was not about, and thus the opportunity to liberate from her tyrannical rule a piece of cake or a pie was not to be lost. Quickly casting my eye around the shelves for a convenient morsel, I saw a treasure trove. There, neatly rowed up on a high shelf were a dozen large bottles of lemonade. Time being of the essence, for I might at any moment be discovered, I seized a bottle and quickly unscrewed the top, Without more ado, I tip-tilted my head back, pointed my nose at the ceiling and chug-a-lugged nearly a half-pint of straight gin. Mother had sabotaged Warnie's gin, removing a goodly quantity and making up the deficit with water. However, her waste-not, want-not nature forbade her throwing the expensive spirit away, and she concealed it in plain sight, disguised as innocuous soft drink. In so doing, she had nearly sabotaged me also, for it was quite some time before my eyes stopped watering, and I felt decidedly peculiar for a considerable while. It was my own fault, of course, first for my natural boy's larceny and second because the incongruity of seeing lemonade in the larder should have warned me. It was not the sort of thing that ever would, under normal circumstances, have been bought at The Kilns, for the artificiality of such products was universally despised by all the adult members of the household.

Time passed, and Jack and Mother cared each for the other and both for Warnie, and Warnie for both of them.

Warnie spent most of his time at work in his study, down the long dark corridor past Mother's bedroom in the new wing of the house; the haunted room at the end of that wing was once again relegated to the role of store-room, and it was there that Warnie kept his bottles of ginger cordial, a drink of eye-watering potency which he used as a substitute for alcohol and which he often shared with me. Mother and Jack spent as much of their time as possible together. Jack worked in his study while Mother rested. Evenings they sat together in the common room and read, played Scrabble, read aloud to each other or talked. Sometimes, they merely sat in companionable silence. Many times I would run down to the Ampleforth Arms, taking two empty quart screw-top bottles and would return with half a gallon of draught bitter beer. I would take Jack and Mother two pint tankards of polished pewter and a half-pint glass mug for myself, together with the bottles of beer, and I would sit with them for as long as it took for me to drink my half; then I would leave them to pursue my own interests in the woods or wherever. Jack would wash out the bottles and tankards hours later, before he went to bed.

Once, I carried the ale to the common room to find them both sitting still, tears rolling down their faces. Alarmed, I cried out, "What's wrong? What's the matter?" "Nothing's wrong, Doug," said Jack, smiling through his tears. "We're reading the poems of A. E. Housman and they always do this to us." I poured the beer and left them, not understanding the strange way in which the recognition of great beauty can bring tears. I am older now, but I still have not read the poems of A. E. Housman.

Jack occasionally suffered from a recurrent condition which caused one side of his face, the left, to swell up below the jawbone and to cause him excruciating pain. I think it must have been a blocked or infected salivary gland and is probably a quite treatable condition. However, Jack's "golf ball," as he jokingly called it, was untreated and it reappeared about once a year. I can still see Jack, tears of agony rolling down his face, a delicious meal spread before him as he sat at the dining table, totally incapable of eating, the pain caused by attempting to do so being too severe. He laughed ruefully and said, "It's probably very good for me," referring to his awkward predicament. Jack enjoyed his food with great gusto and liked nothing better than to sit down to a fine dinner amidst the people he loved and eat, converse, discuss and enjoy an evening celebration of the gifts of God.

Mother and Jack took us on a trip to Solva in the summer of 1959, that fast, flashing time. We went by train, the use of British Railways being a ghastly mistake. Jack, in pain from his own illness (osteoporosis), worried sick about Mother's ability to stand a day at the mercy of the impersonal tyranny of the railway system of the time, and subject to the constant bickering of two bored and irritable schoolboys, became irascible as the long, wearisome day progressed. British Railways at that time struck me as a sort of huge malevolent tangle of rails, governed by bored and for the most part incompetent bureaucrats, and run by insolent and idle men whose main occupation seemed to be trying to find a reason, any reason, to down tools and "go out on strike"; the small man's modern method of exerting power for power's sake. The crews of the trains themselves seemed to regard passengers as a barely necessary evil, an unpleasant intrusion whom they were compelled, albeit reluctantly, to tolerate. A four-hour drive by car became a day-long purgatory for Jack and Mother at the hands of British Railways. Finally, upon reaching Haverford-West (after the last few hours had been spent in a non-corridor train), both Jack and I made good speed towards a sign which read GENTLEMEN. This need attended to, we all climbed into an aged taxi for the last ten or twelve miles to Solva, and to the Ship Inn.

Mother had told Jack only of the charm of the Ship and nothing of its shortcomings. It was an old building, full of low ceilings, narrow and (for Mother) difficult staircases and spartan accommodations. Jack, tired, irritable and disappointed, was, for the only time I ever witnessed, actually angry with Mother. She had brought him all this way at, he knew, great expense to her own stamina to a dingy, uncomfortable hotel in the middle of nowhere. The night was mole-tunnel black with the tangible, wet velvet darkness of the Welsh valleys thick throughout the village. But after a few short, sharp words, Jack stormed out for a walk. Within a few minutes, the ancient sorcery of Solva had seduced him, and he climbed the Cwm behind the village and watched the furtive moon flit out from behind the high, hasting clouds to smile briefly down at the little harbour, the fishing boats standing out against the dark of the water like gulls bobbing on a sunlit sea, the scents of the wild heather, the fennel and the sea lavender surrounding him in the hillside air. A few minutes of this sensory assault and Jack, like all who visited Solva in those days, was caught—trapped by the magic of the Faerie nature of the place. He strode back down the narrow path of the Cwm, the bracken and the brambles clutching at his trousers like the thin fingers of mischievous elves. Soon he was back at the Ship and, after a somewhat sheepish apology to Mother, was busily unpacking with the excitement of a small boy. Later that evening, he sat in the bar, pint in one hand, pipe in the other, with good food beneath his belt and listened to the natural harmony of the Welsh fishermen singing their songs of Wales and the sea. His face was alight with life and love.

The Solva holiday was a great success for both Mother and Jack, but although I often returned later, after Mother's death, Jack never did. For him, the memories would have been too painful. I was last there in July of 1983. I shan't go again. The English have "touristed" the place, the fishermen are gone and even the ghosts of the Druids have left Solva now. How I loathe the way time steals away the glories and the joys of one's childhood, taking even the bittersweet and leaving only dross in its place.

There were fine, happy, wonderful times in this, Mother's personal *entre-guerre*, period; the weeks, the seasons— they seem in my mind not to be separated but to be all part of just one long but all too short interlude.

I remember the long summer days, Mother sitting out in the gardens with Jack or sometimes up at the side of the lake. The green of England's summer foliage was as bright and glowing as the halo of a saint. Summer days of quiet and softness, the occasional vivid electric blue flash of Halcyon himself lending credence to the old phrase of description often used to convey the peculiar quality of stillness and peace which haunts the woods of England in such hours. The winters were no less wonderful, the thick fogs, shot through with the smell of coal smoke, the clear crystal-sharp nights lit by a moon as pale as the Snow Queen's brow. When the lake froze as hard as stone and I skated alone in the moonglow, the trees all glittering with crystals of frost so large that they seemed to have grown special white foliage to celebrate the harsh breath of the winters' nights, I skated on skates that Jack and Warnie had used when they were boys in Ireland and I felt the beauty of those nights wash through me and soak into my very being.

Alone, gliding swiftly across the ice, the only sound that of my blades, I was for a while completely and utterly happy.

There was a time we invited all the neighbours around for a Guy Fawkes night party. Weeks I spent building a huge bonfire, collecting pyrotechnical delights and in deepest secrecy constructing the effigy to be burnt in the traditional way. We served copious quantities of rum punch to ward off the chill on that November 5th night and began to entertain our guests with the beautiful collection of fireworks. Somehow, the lid of the large wooden chest containing the neatly stacked fireworks was left open, and a St. Catherine's wheel, breaking free of its restraint, hurled itself into the midst of the box. Seldom have I seen a more dramatic display; the simultaneous eruption of skyrockets, Roman candles, flying saucers, thunderclaps, untethered St. Catherine's wheels—a dozen or more of each, and others besides—hurling up into the air in all directions, provided a staggering sight. A few of the guests had to dive for cover, but that merely added to the fun. The bonfire was huge and the "Guy," loaded with still more rockets and Vesuvius fountains, burnt with great gusto. Jack told me later that our Guy had been a little too realistic for his taste and had rather upset both him and Warnie, reminding them both of their experiences during the First World War. Warnie voiced his agreement with Jack, and I never built a Guy again.

Carol singers came around at Christ's Mass, and we served them hot, steaming rum punch, too. Mother had found the recipe in some old Elizabethan tome at the Bodleian or somewhere, and it contains some unlikely ingredients. However, it tastes delicious and, as one of the carol singers remarked (with a slight cough) after he tasted it, "Bah gum, that'll keep aht the cold and even if it doan't, it'll put enough 'airs on yer chest ter do it for yer." The carol singers were a group organised by a neighbour, one Dr. Clarke, and they sang very well, in fine harmony. I think they collected money for the Oxford Committee for Famine Relief.

I loved the snow of these winters, too, and risked my neck on various slopes nearby on everything from a tin tray to a borrowed toboggan. Inside The Kilns all was warmth and comfort. Though the house was now centrally heated, a fire of coal burned in the common room, the dining room, Warnie's study and often in Mother's bedroom. The common room had the only open fireplace; all the others had controlled combustion stoves. These had little windows of mica in their doors, through which one could see the state of the fire, and they burnt "ovoids" made of coal dust and some form of bonding agent. They were so-called smokeless fuel.

I was often asked to go out to the old kilns and get a scuttleful of coal, not a job I enjoyed—not so much because of the cold, dark nights in which any kind of bogle might be prowling, but because the floor of the old kilns was often littered with bricks or pieces of brick which had fallen from the chimneys high above. I would dash into the darkness of the kiln, scuttle poised at the ready, plunge it into the heap of coal or ovoids stored within, and dash back out again, hoping that any loose bricks would not choose that moment to tumble. There were many little chores that I did around the house. When Paxford was away, I even took charge of the grumpy old Aga and the central-heating boiler. We became a family. It didn't happen all at once, but slowly and surely Jack and Warnie and I were building some sort of relationship. I could never claim to have been anywhere near as important to Jack as he was to me, but I really do believe that I did become important to him.

In addition, I began to understand a little about Jack

and began to be able to see the enormous wealth of compassion in him. On one warm summer afternoon, two local urchins came running to the house, terrified, and said that they had found the body of a man up on the hill. Jack immediately put on his hat and went to investigate (declining, much to my relief, my suggestion that I should accompany him). His feelings of apprehension and his dislike of the very idea of going to examine a possible corpse can be imagined. However, he did not, as so many of us would, simply pass the buck, but went himself to find out what was the truth behind the incoherent babblings of these two obviously badly frightened little boys. It turned out that the corpse was a young man fast asleep; he had been out all night and was a recent patient of a psychiatric institution and, furthermore, he had no money. I saw Jack walking down past The Kilns with this fellow, deep in earnest conversation, his face lit with warmth and compassion. Jack took him down to the bus stop and put him on a bus for Oxford, with five or ten pounds in his pocket, and returned to the house to resume his daily routine.

Another illustration of Jack's compassion and understanding can be found in a trivial (although to me very important) episode which occurred on a chilly autumn afternoon during this period. I had been given a kayak as a present and dearly loved it. Made of a light wooden frame, covered with P.V.C. fabric, it was a delicate and very lively little craft. I soon became adept at hurtling around the lake and even paddling standing up. Soon after I was given this beautiful boat, Jack and Mother came walking up to the lake one afternoon while I was paddling to and fro. Much to my surprise, Jack, after watching for a moment or two, hailed me and asked me to ferry him across the lake. I must confess that, thrilled though I was to be asked, I also felt some considerable nervousness at the thought that this exercise might well end with both Jack and me taking an involuntary plunge into the icy-cold water, for Jack's sense of equilibrium was not the best, and even the process of entering a kayak is fraught with unpleasant possibilities, particularly for the inexperienced. Jack himself must have been a great deal more apprehensive than I was, but such was his understanding of how much pleasure this simple thing would give me that he took his courage in hand and stepped into the unstable canoe and immediately sat down (which, by the way, is the *only* way to get into a kayak). With a few careful strokes of the double paddle, I soon had us pointed out towards the middle of the lake and we swiftly and silently glided across the still, mirror-smooth water. Jack looked about him with an air of real pleasure and remarked, "Well, Doug, this is delightful." He went on to remark on how much daintier and more like a real water creature the canoe was than were the punts to which he was accustomed. When we reached the far bank, a matter of only a few seconds, Jack simply stood up and stepped ashore. "Thanks, Doug," he said. "I can see why you're so fond of her. She's a wonderful craft." I glowed in the warmth of his praise and approval, for by then I loved and respected Jack and to win his approbation gave me a rush of happiness. Jack risked a ducking in a cold lake simply to please a rather too cocksure boy because he knew that in so doing he would make both me and Mother very happy.

Jack never preached at me, never tried to push me in any any religious direction, but if I had a question, he would take great pains to answer it as clearly as he could. Furthermore, he would take the time to consider the problem and then, having thought, he would answer carefully and concisely. I doubt whether any of my insignificant schoolboy dilemmas gave him pause for as long as a split second, but Jack had the compassion to pause and think, or at least to seem to, before replying, thus giving the impression that my affairs were of sufficient (a) importance and (b) difficulty to require thought.

The year 1956 began in happiness and tranquillity and saw the beginnings of a sense of personal security evolving within me as the atmosphere of a settled, warm and loving home began to develop at 10 Old High Street. The summer of 1956 was one of long, warm evenings, ripe plums on the fruit trees and a burgeoning vegetable garden. By December, the plug had been pulled, and all the joy, security and happiness drained away, leaving me a bewildered and frightened little boy, alone to face the world. Had I not met Jesus in the churchyard that day, I don't think I could have retained any grip on reality at all.

Nineteen-fifty-seven was the year of Mother's renaissance and the quiet miracle of her return to health and the visible, almost tangible growth of a huge love between her and Jack. It grew from the more conventional love of a man for a woman and a woman for a man, until it became something indescribable in human terms, a great and holy glorification of God's gift to mankind. For me, 1957 was time to take stock, to settle again into a wary pattern of hope and to be warmed (and I was) by the glow of love that Mother and Jack showered around them. It was also a year of establishing new friendships—with Warnie, with Fred Paxford and with The Kilns.

The year 1958 was the one of The Kilns rejuvenation: new carpets, new paint, new furniture, replanned gardens and joy, comfort for mind and body, Mother and Jack revelling in this unexpected gift of time deliberately given to them (and to me) by God, both realising that it was unlikely to last for very long. A year of guests and outings for Mother after being so long confined; a year of once again building some sense of security and safety.

Nineteen-fifty-nine began in a haze of happiness and joy for all of us; that summer there was Solva with Jack and Mother and they went to Ireland together while I was at school. I had grown up considerably since 1956 and I was becoming more independent. For all that, I still spent much time with Mother and Jack and grew closer to Warnie, too. The end of this year brought darkness with it, however, as Mother's disease began a new offensive, and although at first radiation therapy seemed able to control this new attack, the enemy was slowly but steadily gaining in strength and Mother was faltering. Jack, Warnie and I began to avoid each other's eyes for fear of seeing each other's fear.

CHAPTER 13

The Thread Snaps

I was fourteen years old, or near enough to it, and Jack and Mother despaired of my ever achieving any scholastic success at Dane Court. Somehow, and I never did find out how, they heard of a school called Lapley Grange, at Machynlleth in Montgomeryshire, a beautiful county in my beloved Wales. Lapley Grange was what we called a "crammer," a school designed and run to assist problematic students to pass the Common Entrance to Public Schools examinations. The Headmaster, Ivor M. Cross, became my equivalent of Kirkpatrick, the man who had tutored Jack in his youth, and whom Jack had immortalised as "Kirke," the young hero Digory of *The Magician's Nephew*, who becomes the old Professor in *The Lion, the Witch and the Wardrobe*. He and his wife ran the school with a staff of talented and intelligent teachers who were dedicated to their profession. Both Mr. and Mrs. Cross were brilliant teachers and had a deep understanding of children. Lapley was a small school; the total number of pupils when I arrived there was thirty-three—thirty-one boys and two little girls, Joan and Annette, whom I grew very fond of and loved to tease.

I began my year at Lapley badly. Mother and Jack came to see me off at Bicester railway station. Mr. Cross was on the train with a group of boys coming down from London for the beginning of the term. I was excited and keenly looked forward to living in Wales. I said good-bye to Jack and Mother and boarded the train. I put my case on the luggage rack and went to wave at the window in a gesture of farewell. I leaned out of the open window just as the train began to move, and looked back at Jack and Mother, standing without me on the platform. They were both looking towards me and smiling, but I saw them surrounded by a strange brightness, a light glowing phenomenon, outside of which was a blackness, a sort of dark shadowy emptiness. Suddenly, with no warning and for no discernible reason, I was hit hard by a solid mass of fear, so palpable that it was as if I had been hit on the head with a brick. I felt a wave of doom, like a savage blow, wash over me and, white-faced and shaking, I took my seat in the train. Fear went with me to Wales and was my unwelcome companion for several weeks. That train journey was a nightmare; I was not afraid of being away from home, for, after all, I had spent the last six years or more at boarding school in term time and all over the country in holidays. I was not afraid of the unfamiliarity of a new school. I had long ago evolved the undefeatable attitude that "the worst they can do is kill me, and that might well lead to an improved life-style anyway." I was terrified that I would never see my mother again. I was wrong, but the longer I sat in that train the more oppressed and afraid I felt. I was holding my tears in check only barely and by considerable exertion of will by the time we reached Lapley Grange.

Lapley is a place of stunning beauty, high on the side of a hill overlooking the Dyfi estuary. The house is built on a flat place cut into the living rock of the hillside, a forecourt in front of the house is faced with a battlemented stone wall, upon which in summer one could sit and stare out across the Dyfi valley and breathe the rich air of Wales.

Azaleas and rhododendrons covered the hillside beneath, and swallows darted past one's head in pursuit of their airborne prey.

My first week there was spent in almost constant tears; all the years of training that big boys don't cry, keep a stiff upper lip and so forth simply dissolved, washed away by the tide of misery engendered by the fear that Mother was going to die while I was far away from her. Some of the other boys made kind and valiant attempts to cheer me, but I could not tell them of my terror. Finally, Mr. and Mrs. Cross decided that this had gone on long enough and that they had better talk to me. I was summoned to see them. "Now, then," said Mr. Cross sternly, "what's all this about?" I blurted out, "Sir, my mother's got cancer and I'm afraid that she's going to die and that I'll never see her again." "Nonsense," he replied. "She came to the station to see you off, didn't she? You can't get about like that if you've got cancer!" It was the only time that I ever knew him to be completely wrong about anything. Mrs. Cross took a softer line of approach. "You're just worried about what's going to happen to you here," she said soothingly. "We're just here to help you, you know; nothing is going to happen to your mother." That was the only time I ever knew her to be wrong about anything. Time—time and exhaustion—eventually brought me out of my self-pity and premature grief. The first thing I should learn, Mr. Cross decided, was how to write. And so, I began by copying, hour after hour, carefully designed script, over and over again. Soon I had learnt not only to write, but to write legibly, and when Mother's letters, full of news of The Kilns and the doings of its denizens began to arrive regularly, I began to relax. Furthermore, even during my first few months there, I began to learn.

James (Jimmy) Nuthall, who had been at Dane Court with me and had been a friend, was already at Lapley and so I had at least one familiar face. Soon I began to build up a friendship, on at least a superficial level, with some of the other boys, "Jo-Jo" Cotterell, for example; a lad of great good will with whom I got on extremely well. For the first time in my life, I actually began to enjoy school. By the time the first term was halfway through, I began to feel that I had a place at Lapley and I began to notice and take heed of the countryside which surrounded this safe haven. The whole of that area of Wales is magnificent, dramatic hill country; the steep-sided hills of bright grass and joyful wild flowers are broken here and there by brutal outcroppings of stark grey rock. There are valleys so precipitous that one might better term them ravines, through which tumble garrulous streams, gaily cascading down and down over leaps and falls to join at last the Dyfi River and there to lose their own ebullient identity amidst the sluggish waters of the tidal estuary. The little Welsh sheep dot the landscape like small bundles of agile and wary thistledown, scampering away at one's approach, the ewes calling urgently to their lambs to follow swiftly to safer ground, away from these intrusive bi-pedal interlopers. We used to go for long walks through this wonderful land and hurled ourselves down grassy slopes, soldiers of France falling to the glory of Napoleon, or more often heroes slaughtered in the line of duty in the Second World War. And I forgot to fear. I went home for my first holiday from Lapley bursting with accounts of where we had gone and what we had done and how much I was enjoying my new school. My enjoyment was reflected in my reports, too, for at last I was becoming a student to whom learning itself was becoming important. These teachers managed to make their pupils aware that they had a priceless gift to impart and so, with their skills and talent and my own new willingness, I began to learn and to enjoy learning.

In England, the school year was divided into three terms—spring, summer and winter. They varied in length but I cannot remember by how much. My first term at Lapley soon ended, and gave way to the so very important holidays.

My second term was better than my first. During those holidays, Mother had seemed well, and the slight cloud of apprehension which drifted aimlessly about The Kilns was not enough to dispel my enthusiasm for my new environment. Of the second holidays from this school I remember little other than that it was then that fear began to cloud once again the summer skies of my mind. I had been made a Prefect and returned eventually for my third and last term with mixed emotions. Selfishly, I was glad to get away from The Kilns, for by the beginning of that summer term of 1960 the miasma of fear and the constant, unspoken awareness of pain, Jack's, Warnie's and Mother's, made home an oppressive place. I was so involved with my own feelings that I could not wait to turn my back on all of them and run away to Wales, to Lapley, where I could forget. Perhaps I had simply had enough of misery and was tired of fear. Anyway, I looked forward, for the first time in my life, to school rather than home, but at the same time I also felt guilty that I was going to a place where I would enjoy myself and deliberately not think about home and all the woes attached to it. Also, I still carried my own share of fear for Mother, beaten down and subdued as it was. That summer of 1960 saw the best of my schooldays. I had established myself as an identity and had a place in a compact and tightly knit society. I returned to Lapley that term as Deputy Head Prefect and soon was promoted to

Head Prefect. Better still, the teachers began to trust me in the classroom and to invite my participation in discussions and explanations. Sometimes, if another student was experiencing difficulties in understanding some point or other which I had already managed to grasp, one of these gifted educators might say, "Gresham, how would you explain it?" I would convert my understanding of the teacher's explanation into schoolboy jargon and thus together we would get the message across. This ensured that I learnt more thoroughly and so did the other student. I was by no means singled out for this sort of thing; many of us were asked from time to time to help explain things to each other. For me, however, this technique opened a whole new door to the world of learning; hitherto, I had always been talked *at* by teachers; never before had I been invited actually to become involved in the process of education, my own or anyone else's. Indeed, that last term at Lapley was the crowning glory of my schooldays, and the end of it saw the end of my childhood.

I have many beautiful memories of that summer: long bicycle rides through the hills of Montgomeryshire, part of my job as Head Prefect being to ride up and down the long line of cyclists to ensure that strict order was kept, to assist any younger child to make repairs in the case of a puncture and then to encourage him to catch up with the rest of the school; walks to Talybont, over the hillsides and down the slatey shepherds' paths, to arrive in the village hot and thirsty, have a strawberries-and-cream tea, and then head back across the mountains. We swam in a natural rock-pool in one of the hurried, leaping streams which cut through the hills. I remember a trip to Tywyn to play on the sands of the beaches, and I found a boxer pup there, or she found me, and at once she and I were wrestling and romping amongst the dunes. Jo-Jo Cotterell, whose parents had taken him and me on this outing, ran round and round us exhorting the dog to demolish me. In truth, she needed little encouragement, for the powerful sweeps of her paws, for which the breed is named, although all in play, were raising red weals on my back and chest. But very soon her owner appeared—a lovely girl of perhaps eighteen, brown as a berry and dressed in only a brief bikini—and took her dog very firmly in charge. That chance encounter was to begin a lifelong affection for boxers. Aside from trips with school friends and the school en masse, there were trips with Jean Wakeman, who occasionally drove down to Wales to take me out for a treat. She would talk to innkeepers and make notes for her work, and I would roam about.

Alone, I haunted the heights of Cader-Idris, wandered the banks of Llyn-Tal-y-Llyn, climbed among the crags of Plynlymon, chasing the ancient Welsh shadows through the mists. Is it any wonder that a part of me still flits about those moody mountains of Wales, together with the shade of Owen Glendwr, that ancient fighter for the freedom of the Welsh?

I sat and passed, with an unusually high average mark, the C.E. exams, and as soon as I heard the results I went to Mr. Cross and asked him if Mother had been told of my success. He assured me that she had.

The morning of Monday the 20th of June was a gleaming, bright morning, warm and welcoming, but the glow of the sun held a feeling of intangible menace. I noticed that there was unusual activity about the school-yard. The Crosses' Rover car was prepared for a journey, and Greville Cross, who was a student with us, was called out of class by his mother, who walked up and down in the courtyard talking earnestly to him. The day grew brighter with that strange glowing sunlight that seems to presage doom and makes the brilliance of the glowing flowers all the brighter. Suddenly, inexplicably, I knew that all of this concerned me. I did not have to send to the village to find out for whom the bell tolled. It was no surprise when Mr. Cross came to fetch me and told me gently and kindly that he had received a telegram to say that Mother was desperately ill and that I was to go home at once. Mr. Cross and the Lapley Grange chauffeur/handyman drove me all the way home to The Kilns. I sat in the back seat in miserable silence all the way from Wales to Oxford. When we arrived, they tactfully refused my offer of tea and left at once, leaving me with Jack and Warnie. For the second time, I went to bid my mother good-bye.

The first thing she said was "Doug, congratulations on passing your Common Entrance examinations." I held her in my arms and merely wept. I was now taller than she would have been had she been able to stand, but as usual it was she who comforted me. Again I walked that path, from The Kilns, down alongside the stone wall, to the wrought-iron churchyard gate. I lifted the latch and stepped once more into His presence. Again I was told that if I really could not survive without my mother's help and support, once again I could ask and it would be granted, but deep inside, where our honesty lives caged, I knew that now, at the age of fourteen, I could make it, somehow, and I also felt that to ask for the same miracle twice would be presumptuous. I looked around the churchyard at the glowing trees and the quiet, sleeping stones. I said aloud, "Thy will be done," and I walked out of the churchyard and home to the empty and desolate Kilns.

CHAPTER 14

Joy, Jack and Sorrow

THE YEAR 1959 was, for Mother and Jack, the year of their time together. They had climbed from the depths of despair and had built happiness from the ashes of a promise. In 1959 they reached the pinnacle of that happiness and began their descent. Mother was fit and well for almost all of the year and revelled in being so; she played her role of Mrs. Lewis with pride and pleasure, a true wife to Jack in every way. By September, Mother's ever-present aches and pains had begun to become worse, and by October it was evident that the axe was poised; cancerous growth was detected once again in Mother's bones and once again she and Jack had to face the inevitability of her impending departure. Warnie, on hearing the news, was grief-stricken and soon anaesthetised by gin. Jack and Mother cared for him, and it was not long before he recovered. They didn't tell me, probably for my own sake, but such reticence is always a mistake. In my case, doubly so, for I did not have to be told; I could feel the worry, the sorrow and the fear and I resented the fact that I was not told at once exactly what was happening. Mother and Jack had visited Eire together and Jack had proudly shown Mother all his old haunts and had taken her to meet Arthur

Greeves. They brought back with them a painting which Arthur had done for them of an Irish barley field. I have it to this day.

Mother had loved her trip to Ireland and had but one major ambition left. She longed to visit Greece, that magic land whence the old gods had come, and to which they had all been banished long ago to hide, forsaken and forgotten, amongst the aged olive trees and the dark caves, the taste of heroes' blood but a long-gone memory. Jack also longed to see the sacred groves and the scented pines through which the gibbering wraiths of ancient myths flitted and grieved for the passing of their time. However, Jack was sorely afraid. He feared that the ordeal of travelling would be too much for Mother. When he consulted Warnie, the advice from his brother was to take the risk and go. After all, he pointed out, if Mother's remaining time was so limited, should they not make the best possible use of what was to be granted to them?

An old pupil and long-time friend of Jack's, Roger Lancelyn Green and his wife, June, accompanied a party to Greece in April of 1960, and that tour-party included Mother and Jack. The trip was a huge success for both Jack and Mother, largely through the efforts of Roger and June Lancelyn Green, who went to enormous trouble to take extra care of Mother and when her pain became apparent, Roger adopted the technique of plying her with retsina. Imagine Jack right in the middle of the home of the ancient Greek myths and legends, quaffing retsina, the same heady resin-flavoured wine that has been drunk there for centuries. They climbed the Acropolis and, seated on the marble, looked down upon the desecration that is modern Athens. Mother was performing prodigious feats for one whose body was yet again fast becoming a battlefield of dead and dying tissues falling before the onslaught of her disease. Jack's pure and almost pagan delight in the haunted ruins and the Attic hills was tempered only by his concern for Mother's well-being, a concern which grew as the days passed to a constant nagging anxiety. Also, of course, he had his own aches and pains to contend with. They were away twelve days, twelve days in which Warnie and I shared our loneliness, each with the other, and so overcame it. I joined him after dinner in the study for a glass of ginger cordial each evening, and thus the days soon passed.

The day that Mother and Jack came home, the 14th of April, I learnt two things. The first was obvious as soon as Mother sat down in the common room, and that was that the trip had drained her of almost all of her last remaining strength. She was utterly exhausted, but glowing with the joy of where she had been and what she had seen. The second lesson that I learnt that day was of more long-term significance, for it pointed out a major difference in character between Mother and Jack and made me realise for the first time that Jack was probably a better person than Mother was, in one way, at least. You shall judge for yourself.

It was at Mycenae that Mother, at the limits of her endurance, decided that the famous lion gate was as far as she could manage to walk. She told Jack that she could go no further and suggested that she sit and rest and that he go on with the rest of the party. Jack, of course, would have none of this and said that, as he was tired himself, he would sit with her and await the return of the rest of the party from the ruins at the top of the hill. Jack sat down, his heart aching for love of his Joy, his pride in her achievements, and his concern for her. A typical middle-aged, over-painted, over-weight tourist lady (perhaps jealous of all the attention lavished upon Jack and Mother) came puffing up

the hill. Upon seeing that Mother and Jack had given up
the idea of ascending to the top of the hill and had stopped
to rest, she took the opportunity to make a snide comment.
"Well!" she said, "you didn't get very far, did you?" Jack's
iron self-control bent for a split second. "Oh, go and have a
heart attack!" he snapped. This lady sniffed, raised her nose
like a banner, followed it up the hill and, upon reaching the
top, did precisely that! Jack and Mother, still sitting,
resting, saw her carried down on a stretcher. Mother
related this tale to me with a certain relish and enjoyment,
almost with glee. Jack, on the other hand, was filled with
horror and remorse. He felt deeply ashamed and guilty;
whilst Mother's attitude was that it served the old bitch
right, Jack's was that for him to wish ill upon another
human being was a deeply shameful act and he was
embarrassed and hurt by Mother's telling of the tale. He
made her promise never to mention it again.

Mother rested and regained some of her strength, but it
was apparent that she was never to return to the health she
had so recently enjoyed. On the 21st of June, the great axe
Labrys, the ceremonial axe of royal execution in the Court
of Minos of Crete, swung at Mother and she became
desperately ill. She was taken to the Acland Nursing Home
to die, and I was brought home from school to spend her
last days close to her. Labrys of Minos missed, and again
Mother fought off that dark, evil shadow. Within a week,
she was home in a wheelchair. I remember Jack pushing
her around the drive of The Kilns. She looked deathly ill, as
indeed she was, but she glowed with the pleasure of seeing
again the flowers and trees and she looked about her like a
small child seeing such things for the first time. I, walking
beside her, in my child's cruel lack of understanding, felt
embarrassed for her, embarrassed by her so obvious joy at
such little things. A painter was up on a ladder, working on·

the window frame of Jack's study, "Hello," Mother called out gaily. The painter started and, hurriedly transferring his paintbrush to his left hand, clumsy, for it already held a pot of paint, attempted to hold on to the ladder, the paint pot and the paintbrush all at once with his left hand while he touched his cap with his right hand. "Arternoon, Ma'am," he said and quickly returned to work. "Oh," said Mother absently, "I thought that was Paxford." Inwardly, I writhed with embarrassment. Mother smelt the roses, watched the gently swaying silver birches and delighted once more in the beauty of God's creations. Gratefully, I went back to school in Wales, happy to escape the sickness of The Kilns, and, though it shames me to have to admit it, the pitying glances, the overheard "Ain't it a shame though . . . ." and the general embarrassment of having a dying mother.

I went back to Lapley, but I knew that this time there would be no reprieve on my account, for, you see, I had once again walked through Quarry churchyard. On the 14th of July, once again the brightness and the shining shadows of endings hung over Lapley Grange. The car was readied for a journey, and I knew that Labrys had swung again and this time had not missed. Gently, and with great kindness, Mrs. Cross told me that Mother had died during the night and I was to go home at once. At first, I felt numbness, and then grief, of course, but mixed with the overpowering sense of loss was a strange feeling of huge relief. Now, at least, her pain was over, but, in truth, more important to me was the fact that my long fear-filled time of waiting was finished. The blow had fallen and I need wake in dread no longer.

This second drive from Wales to Oxford saw a very different reaction from me. The first time, I had been silent and withdrawn, saying barely a word all the length of that trip, but on this second drive, I talked incessantly with Mrs. Cross, who accompanied me this time. We discussed in great detail the history of the Second World War. I asked question after question. I did not want to think about what ordeal might be awaiting me at The Kilns. I would face that when I had to and not before. I didn't cry, not then, not outwardly; I chattered and kept my mind filled with everything I could think of to hold back the flood tide of my grief. Twenty-three years later I can't hold it back. Even as I write, my tears fall on the page. For whom do I grieve? For the loss of my mother? Or is it from pity for the little boy that I was? A sort of time-lapse self-pity? I don't know.

When we finally arrived at The Kilns, they dropped me at the front door and again tactfully drove away at once. I walked in through the front door and went to the common-room door. I opened it and saw Jack across the room by the fireplace. He was facing me, his left hand on the mantelpiece. His appearance shocked me; I had last seen him merely ten days or so previously, but since that time he had aged twenty years or more. His eyes held the look of a soul in Hell. My brittle shell smashed, and I broke. "Oh, Jack," I burst out, and then the tears came. Jack rushed across the room and put his arm around me. I held on to him, as we both wept. That was the only occasion upon which any physical demonstration of our love for each other ever occurred. "Jack," I finally said, "What are we going to do?" He looked at me, his compassion for me showing through his own grief. "Just carry on somehow, I suppose, Doug," he replied; and so this we set out to do. After a while, I went out into the garden and walked over to the hydrangeas behind the willow, which wept along with me. The very beauty of the garden seemed to mock both me and my sorrow. There, Fred Paxford found me. His huge arm gentle around my shoulder, he pulled me to him and said softly, "Doan't cry, son." He had no more words, and so we stood together in mute and mutual sorrow, for Fred, too, loved and respected Mother.

Mother's funeral was held on the following Monday, the 18th of July. Jean Wakeman had come to see me and had told me that, as my friend and support, she expected me to comport myself like a soldier on parade, God bless her! I did not weep at that ceremony, though Austin Farrer's tears as he read the service tested my strength sorely. I stood at attention and held my head high. I remember the sunshine flooding the chapel at the Oxford crematorium and the glimpse of flame as the coffin slid into the roaring furnace behind the curtains. It was a windy, beautiful day and I felt then, as I do now, that God had given Mother a fine and fitting farewell to this world. Seldom since have I seen a better day on which to return one's earthly clay to the planet from which it had sprung. In shock, perhaps, my mind retained no more than that.

I returned to Lapley Grange to perform my final duty of Head Prefect, and through the fog of my memory of those first few days without Mother, I recall that Jean drove me back to Wales. I stood in the Church of Eglysfach and read the lesson: I Corinthians 13.

"Though I speak with the tongues of men and of angels, and have not charity, I am become as sounding brass or a tinkling cymbal. And though I have the gift of prophecy, and understand all mysteries, and all knowledge; and though I have all faith, so that I could remove mountains, and have not charity, I am nothing. And though I bestow all my goods to feed the poor, and though I give my body to be burned, and have not charity, it profiteth me nothing. Charity suffereth long, and is kind; charity envieth not; charity vaunteth not itself, is not puffed up, Doth not behave itself unseemly, seeketh not her own, is not easily provoked, thinketh no evil; Rejoiceth not in iniquity, but rejoiceth in the truth; Beareth all things, believeth all things, hopeth all things, endureth all things. Charity never faileth: but whether there be prophecies, they shall fail; whether there be tongues, they shall cease; whether there be knowledge, it shall vanish away. For we know in part, and we prophesy in part. But when that which is perfect is come, then that which is in part shall be done away. When I was a child, I spoke as a child, I understood as a child, I thought as a child: but when I became a man, I put away childish things. For now we see through a glass, darkly; but then face to face: but then shall I know even as also I am known. And now abideth faith, hope, and charity, these three; but the greatest of these is charity."

That day, I started to become a man. As Jack said, "It is not important to succeed, but to do right. The rest is up to God."

CHAPTER 15

Carrying On

JACK was never again the man he had been before Mother's death. Joy had left him and also, so it seemed, had joy. Strangely, despite the constant worry and fear that Mother's continued life caused him, he needed her. For years now, it had been Mother's strength, wit and courage which had supported all of us, but Jack more than any of us needed her encouragement and her humour to lean upon; and now, how was he to stand her loss without her? Jack's grief was almost tangible; he wore it like a heavy cloak in those first few weeks. What man would, whilst suffering such pain, stop to think that others all around him were suffering like agony, and that almost everyone at some time in his life would suffer such feelings, and that by writing down his feelings and analysing them he might help others to cope with grief? Jack did! He wrote *A Grief Observed*, the title of which completely describes its nature, a book which has helped many people come to grips with the facts of grief. *A Grief Observed* has not been "padded" to make it more acceptable to "everyman," as has been said by a contemporary writer; it is indeed the simple and literal description of Jack's own feelings and his intellectual and logical reactions to those crushing emotional hammer blows. Jack did not pad; the very essence of his writing style is its simplicity and shining clarity. He did not obscure or bend the truth to make it more acceptable; that would have been contrary to his nature. Jack told me himself that one of the greatest things about telling the truth, whether in writing or in speech, is "that you simply can't be caught out," and therefore to tell the truth is the safest course. It is also the easiest course, for it requires no work of invention and no follow-up work of consistency, for the truth is by nature consistent. A *Grief Observed* is true and therefore it is valuable to all who read it. It cost Jack great pain and yet rewarded him with deeper understanding. I find it hard, even to this day, to read, for I was there when he wrote it and I was a part of his agony and he a part of mine.

Swiftly, Jack disposed of almost every direct, tangible reminder of Mother that he could; he gave her clothes to Mrs. Miller, the cook/housekeeper, to dispose of, with the exception of her fur coat, which, at Mother's own request, was passed over to Kay Farrer (I believe her daughter Caroline still has it). Mrs. Miller gave some of Mother's things away, others she kept. One of the servants at The Kilns at that time was a Mrs. Wilkins, who came to the house each day to perform the tasks for which Mrs. Miller had not the time—the dusting, cleaning and vacuuming and so on. Warnie soon dubbed her "the Wilk." The Wilk developed the habit of appearing for work in our house wearing one or another of what had been Mother's favourite blouses, a habit which caused Jack (and me) repeated flashes of pain. This was the first faint shadow of a strange and fearful evil that was to begin to manifest itself in our household.

Being, as I was, the product of the stiff-upper-lip training of English boarding schools, I was horrified at the very idea of breaking down and showing my grief in public, so I shut it up within me, hidden away deep in the darkness of my mind. Jack was not able, or more likely no longer saw the need, to do this, and again and again I watched with horror (unseen by them) as Mrs. Miller would quite deliberately remind Jack of something that Mother had particularly enjoyed. "Oh, Mr. Jack, just look at them roses. Wouldn't Mrs. Lewis 'ave loved them?" And he would then revel in his unashamed and unrestrained sobs as he struggled to say, "Yes, she would." She hid her exhilaration, but I could feel the sense of power and the concealed triumph that she was enjoying within herself. It seemed to give her huge satisfaction to be able to feel that she could rise above her employer and humble him, bring him to uncontrollable tears, and then watch him weep. Several times, I inadvertently watched this trap laid, baited and sprung. Mrs. Miller would dab her eyes with her apron as if she were weeping along with Jack, but I could feel that she was delighting in her newly found power. Over the years, I had become quite fond of Mrs. Miller, but now I began to see a side of her nature which had hitherto remained hidden. I had never even suspected that she could possess what seemed to me to be a large amount of gratuitous cruelty. But this was a mere foreshadowing of what was to come.

It has been said that Jack's years at Cambridge after Mother's death were happy. That is not true. Jack, when in company with his friends and colleagues, was (after a while) again the jovial, witty intellectual they had known for years, but only Warnie and I knew what effort that cost him, and Warnie knew less than I, for Jack was careful with Warnie; I was more invisible. Jack's colleagues and friends never saw him as he turned from waving a cheery good-bye at the door of The Kilns and casting some pearls of a parting witticism to a departing guest; they never watched him suddenly slump, his whole body shrinking like a slowly deflating balloon, his face losing the light of laughter and becoming grey, until he became once more a tired, sick and grieving man, old beyond his years. Even Warnie did not know, but boys are sometimes hard to see, and many times I watched Jack, unseen by him, as he walked, his mind clear, through the pain of his own Gethsemane. On his way to Warnie's study, tray in hand, he would stop, take a deep breath, pull back his shoulders, raise his head and bring his facial expression under control, then, bold and cheerful of countenance, he would step into the study with a glad cry of "Tea, brother." Perhaps it was partly pride on Jack's part that caused him to conceal his grief from his friends, so that they remained ignorant of his true feelings, for none of them had bothered to come to Mother's funeral. I think Jack was hurt by this and felt both bereaved of his wife and betrayed by his friends at the same time. However, Jack saw no reason to inflict his agony on others and cause them to suffer as well, and *A Grief Observed* was published under the pen name N. W. Clerk, until after Jack's death. He could not hide it from me, nor did he try, for I shared his grief. Many a time when approaching him, light-footed as I have always been, I stopped and backed silently away when I saw that he was racked with pain, sometimes physical, sometimes emotional, but too high a matter for me in either case. No-one knew how Jack suffered in those last three years.

I have since read much about Jack; some very good material and some utter rubbish, by those who have claimed that they knew Jack well. Some of them did, some did not, but all were held at a distance after Mother died. Even such rich and generous souls as Roger Lancelyn Green saw only the cheeriness of Jack's demeanour and not the pain. I could not talk to Jack about Mother, for I knew that if I did, he would weep and so also would I, and although now I feel that this might have been good for both of us, then it would have been anathema for me to cry openly, for as an English schoolboy I found it difficult to show my emotions. After all, I had disgraced myself enough at the beginning of my sojourn at Lapley Grange. I have learnt to weep again since then and am no longer ashamed of doing so, but for those years, and many thereafter, my emotions were kept tightly locked away in the vault of my mind.

Time passed, and Jack's pain, although it did not seem to lessen, seemed to become easier for him to live with, as if his mind had grown tougher in order to bear it. However, from the day of Mother's death, Jack's already poor health began to decline more rapidly. His self-neglect while nursing Mother, and, in my opinion, Humphrey Havard's failure accurately to assess his condition and, later, the fact that Jack did not really want to live any longer, all contributed to his physical deterioration. Had he not been worried about Warnie, Jack would probably have died willingly and at once. Jack's steadily deteriorating condition was not discussed with me; no-one told me. But I knew that Jack was ill and that he was unlikely to improve.

My father, Bill Gresham, visited us in 1960 shortly after Mother's death, and I now know that the apparent coolness of my greeting and our subsequent relationship caused him a considerable amount of pain. I regret that; it was not intended. I was an English schoolboy by then, however, and so I shook his hand and said, "How do you do, sir?" In truth, I confess I felt no emotion for him at all. He was a stranger; we could not bridge the gap of the years of separation. We spent considerable time together and became friends, but really that was all. When he left to go back to America and his new family, I missed him less than I did before he had come.

Jack was really the man to whom I looked, in respect

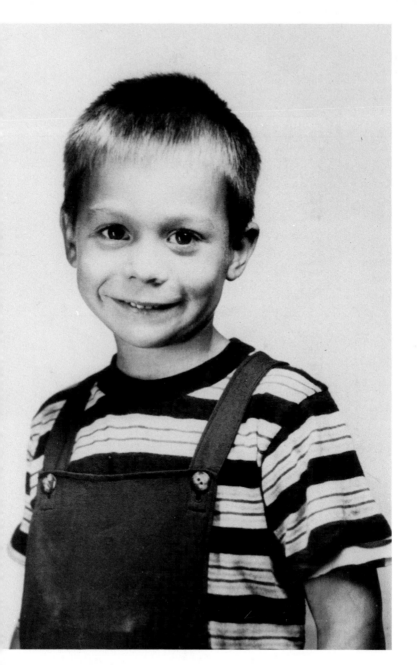

Douglas Gresham in Staatsburg, New York, 1952

C. S. ("Jack") Lewis in The Kilns garden, summer 1957

Joy Lewis and Susie, c. 1957

Joy and Jack, 1958

Joy on the front lawn of The Kilns, c. 1958

Lapley Grange Head Prefect Douglas Gresham, summer 1960

William Lindsay Gresham o[...]
visit to England, summer 196[...]

Fred Paxford, Christmas Day,
1963

Jack, in W. H. ("Warnie") Lewis's study, c. 1961

Chargot, Sir Edward Malet's farm in Somerset

Douglas in Hamburg,
summer 1965

Meredith ("Merrie") Conan-
Davies and "Yogi" (later
Lady Mountevans), 1965

Merrie in London, 1966

Douglas at agricultural college, 1966

Douglas and Merrie's wedding day, 2nd of February, 1967

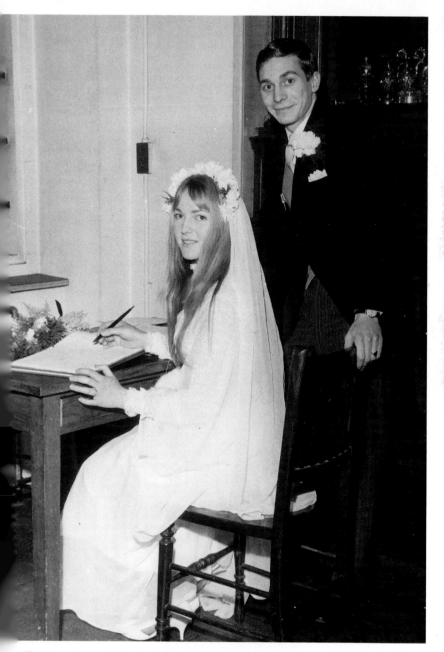

Douglas and Merrie signing the register at Westminster Cathedral

The Greshams' first home
Tasmania—and visitor, 196

Douglas shearing sheep i
South Australia, 1971

Douglas, announcer for radio station 7BU, 1969

James Edward Lindsay Gresham
and his father, Douglas, 1972

The Gresham family, January 1988
From left: Timothy, Douglas
Smoocho (the horse), James
Lucinda (on Smoocho), Merri
and Dominic

and admiration, and, without in the least trying to, he had taken the place in my mind which a father should fill, and it was Jack who, gently and kindly, told me in September of 1962 that my father had taken his own life. Dad had cancer of the tongue, and had no wish to face, or to face his family with, the prospect of a long, ugly death. My feeling for Jack developed from liking and respect through admiration to, at last, some degree of understanding. It was not until quite recently that I realised that I loved Jack, and very deeply at that.

We carried on.

When I was at The Kilns from 1953 onwards, Mrs. Miller was the cook/housekeeper, and Fred Paxford the gardener and handyman. At weekends, when Mrs. Miller was off duty, Fred, as I've said, did the cooking and he was good at it, too. Fred also did all the shopping for the household and kept a strict accounting of every penny he spent; no more honest man ever served his master with greater faith and good will than did Fred Paxford.

Mr. Miller came to the house sometimes to take Mrs. Miller home, but was not at any time while Jack was alive a part of the household. Neither Jack nor Warnie particularly liked Mr. Miller; he was a foreman at the pressed-steel works of Cowley and overly conscious of both the dignity and authority of his position. Mrs. Miller was short, fat and almost bald. In the early years, she was a jolly person, as any good housekeeper should be, but with a will of iron. Eventually, she purchased a wig, and looked the better for it.

When Mother, my brother and I moved into The Kilns, we more than doubled the population of the old house, and it was soon evident that Mrs. Miller would need help to cope with the extra work. The Wilk was therefore found and employed to do the more menial household chores.

After Mother died, in 1960, taking away the main strength of the household, a slow, insidious process began; a process by which, perhaps at first unconsciously, the Millers began to worm their way into The Kilns' daily life. Mr. Miller had progressed from politely waiting in his car, or outside in the garden, to coming inside the kitchen, at first, no doubt, by invitation, but then by habit. He was to be seen more and more often in the kitchen, waiting patiently for his wife to finish her work. Soon he was seated habitually at the table, reading the paper or drinking tea. Mr. Miller was a small, flabby man, with the face of a disappointed spaniel. I believe that, from very early on, he saw possible opportunities for personal gain in the misfortunes of The Kilns and set out to insinuate himself into the household. His first real move was to begin a steady and, in the beginning, almost invisible campaign of silent hostility and ostracism against Fred Paxford. Fred, honest and straightforward countryman that he was, at first was bewildered and then hurt by this and finally became resentful and spent less and less time in the house, keeping more to the garden and to his own little cottage in the grounds, coming in to his rightful place in the kitchen almost only at weekends, when the Millers stayed at home and were not to be seen. Mr. Miller had the habit, when talking, or, to be more precise, when lecturing, for so convinced was he of his own erudition that he rarely spoke in any other manner, of hitching his trousers a little higher on his hips by placing his elbows against his sides and performing a sort of shrug of the shoulders. I have seen a few other men do this and have found myself instantly distrustful of them; the gesture seems to be a physical manifestation of a desire for self-justification in situations of dubious integrity.

I spent much time away in these years, at school or wandering the wilds of Wales on solitary holidays. But it seemed that whenever I took stock of life at home, the Millers were more firmly entrenched at The Kilns. Apart from their steadily deteriorating attitude and behaviour towards Fred Paxford, whose side I took at once, I saw little harm in this phenomenon. Their attitude towards Fred, I realise now, was engendered by the fact that he controlled the household purse. Fred still did the shopping and accounted to "Mr. Jack" for the money spent. The Millers suggested first, to Fred, that he should not have to bicycle around Headington once a week (I often went with him) at his age; they had a car, they could take over the shopping and relieve him of the burden of this onerous chore. I really don't think that Fred saw any ulterior motive behind their offer. I don't think he suspected for one moment that the Millers might have had other than entirely altruistic motives. He refused their offer wholly and solely because he *enjoyed* his shopping trips. They were a regular social event for him; he cycled from shop to shop, chatting with one person after another, and loved every minute of it; it was the highlight of his week. Jack, of course, was well aware of this and when Mrs. Miller, in an offhand way, made the suggestion to Jack, he simply said that Paxford seemed to be doing the job quite adequately, so he might as well carry on doing it. The Millers seemed to think that they were not trusted, by Fred or by Jack, and they hated Fred the more. Jack trusted them, and so did Fred, but I began not to.

As time went on, Jack's condition was not improving; in fact, he was becoming very ill and he cared less and less about the everyday events of the household. He was working hard and grieving hard and his body was at last betraying him. Eventually, he could no longer climb stairs and moved into the common room. He would not use the bedroom where he and Mother had found so much happiness. I moved upstairs into what had been his bedroom and I also took over his upstairs study.

If I must (as I must) shortly relate some of the events and some of the actions of which I am deeply ashamed, I feel that I deserve the luxury of relating one event of which I am inordinately proud. It took place on a chilly night in 1963, or it may have been 1962. Jack and I had retired at about the same time, he to his bed in the common room and I to my upstairs bedroom at the far end of the house. I woke at about two in the morning, not knowing what had awakened me. The moonlight streamed in through the out-jutting dormer window, and I could see my breath steaming as I sat up in bed. Suddenly, I heard a distant sound, the cry of a man in pain or fear! I leapt from my bed and, clad only in my pyjama trousers, I stood in the cold moonlight listening with every fibre of my being, for all the world like a pointing hound. Again I heard the cry of terror, distant but distinct, and coming quite definitely from within the house, and this time I could recognise the voice and discern the words. It was Jack and he was screaming! "Help. Help. Murrrderrr!" came his cry. Frightened I most certainly was, but also determined. Filled with dread, I sprang through the door of the room and into the study, searching as I went for some sort of weapon. The first that caught my eye was what had been one of Mother's sword collection, a Jacobean dress rapier, fancy in the hilt, but of good, sharp steel. I seized this blade, hurled aside the scabbard and flung myself down the stairs and into the common room. Flicking on the light switch with my left hand, I poised myself for action. What a picture I must have made, naked to the waist, sword glittering in my hand, and every muscle tensed and quivering. Jack slowly and complacently emerged from beneath the covers on his bed, rather like a comfortable guinea-pig blinking in the sudden light.

"Jack," I cried out, "what is it? What's the matter?" For besides the two of us, the room was empty. "You were screaming, Jack. I thought you were being murdered."

"Oh, hello, Doug," said Jack. "Nothing really wrong. I was having a nightmare, that's all. I'm sorry if I disturbed you."

By now, he had a twinkle in his eyes, for he had taken in both my attire and my equipment. I asked if I could get him anything and, upon his reply that he didn't think so, I bade him good night, turned off the light and left him. As I gently closed the door, I paused and leaned for a moment or two against the wall, breathing heavily, and despite the night's chill, I found that I was sweating like an excited horse. I went back upstairs, put up my sword and returned to bed, feeling as if I had won my spurs, at least by intent, if not by action. Since then, I have held an armed man at pistol point, and, unarmed, walked in the beams of car headlights to approach a party of intruders carrying high-powered rifles. Nothing has required more of me than that anti-climactic dash to Jack's bedroom.

CHAPTER 16

Magdalen and Applegarth

FROM LAPLEY GRANGE, a school which I enjoyed and at which I was successful, I went to Magdalen College School in Oxford. What a total disaster! I rode my bicycle down Kiln Lane in the cold, drizzlish morning, turned to the left across the Cowley by-pass, then right and down to the Green Road Roundabout. There I turned left again and rode down the London Road towards Headington, through Headington, down Headington Hill and into Oxford. I felt apprehensive about starting the new school. Where should I go? What should I do? And so on. Finally, I arrived at Magdalen and found the bicycle racks. Somehow, I found out where I was supposed to go, and then descended once again into the amorphous mass of banal, brutal idiocy which has been my experience of the basic English school system. I suppose the system was not, in essence, a bad educational structure, for the average, everyday English child; possibly it was merely my misfortune that I did not belong to that category. But then, how could I? I had started my life in America, had been transplanted across an ocean, leaving behind not only everything familiar, but also my father, and crossing a cultural gap itself as wide as that ocean. I had not enjoyed the security and safety that was common to the backgrounds of most of my peers.

My experiences of life were so widely divergent from

those of the boys around me that I could not, nor could I even want to, bridge the gap between their minds and mine. I found almost everything that was said and done at Magdalen either shatteringly boring or amazingly trivial. I did not understand that those unfortunate teachers, with a system developed over centuries of trial and (largely) error, were attempting to prepare the young men in their charge for much of what I had already experienced. I was unable and unwilling to cast aside the lessons I had learned at the hard hands of life itself and return to childhood, and I would not learn to parrot the (to me) meaningless requirements of a formal education. Like the prig that I was, I wasted my time at Magdalen in foolish rebellion and selfish idleness. I caused Jack and Warnie a great deal of unnecessary worry and anguish. I spent my days in idleness, asleep in class (when I got there at all). And my nights? Well, I spent the moonlit ones in the practise of taking game by various nefarious means from the private property of others. It was a game and one from which I derived a great deal of enjoyment. I still think that skillful poaching is a far better sport than mere shooting, for there is the added excitement of the possibility of degrading capture. I have never been caught . . . yet. Other nights, I haunted the streets alone on my bicycle; I helped distressed motorists and longed for friendship and adventure.

Finally, it became evident to Jack and Warnie that Magdalen was of absolutely no use to me, nor I to Magdalen. Jack decided to send me once again to a crammer, this time for the General Certificate of Education exams. It was my intention to go on to an agricultural college, and five ordinary-level G.C.E. passes were required as part of the entry qualifications. The crammer which Jack found for me required a letter of reference from my Housemaster at Magdalen, a man I had met perhaps twice while I had been at the school. I rang his home and he told me to visit him and he would write out the letter. I called at his home and he gave me a glass of sherry, wrote and sealed the letter, and I bade him and Magdalen a relieved farewell. I was duly equipped for my foray out into the world with new clothes and, in due course, arrived at Applegarth, Mark Way, Godalming, Surrey, and a fine sight I must have been, complete with hat and walking stick and still wet behind the ears. I was met by an attractive girl, who answered my ring at the front doorbell. She showed me where to put my case and so forth and told me that her father, Mr. Stevens, one of the partners who ran the school, was away, and that the other partner, Colonel Smitherman, would see me. This tall, rather equine-looking gentleman, with a very colonelish moustache, began my interview with him by telling me what an exceedingly lucky chap I was to have been accepted into his "oh, so exclusive" school, because my Housemaster had written me a very poor reference, and the school had only allowed my presence to endanger its reputation because "your stepfather is who he is." I reflected to myself that he could hardly have managed to be anyone else and at once wrote this man off in my mind as a fool, an opinion which I had reinforced on several occasions and have never had any reason to change. However, the good colonel was not directly involved with me in any way, for he did not teach me and an incident soon occurred which caused him to avoid me assiduously.

I soon became friendly with the Stevens family, and Jill, the girl who met me at the door, I adored at once and have ever since. One wet, dark night, Jill was about to make the final rounds of the school buildings to ensure that all the lights were out and all the windows and doors were secured. This was usually performed by Mr. Stevens, but he was either away or indisposed on this occasion. Anyhow, Jill was about to set out into the darkness and, being a little nervous, asked me if I would accompany her, or I may have volunteered; I'm not sure. The two of us, chatting amicably, proceeded to check the buildings, turning off lights and shutting windows here and there. One of the buildings had a sort of small vestibule in which the light switches were located, and this room was of course pitch black. Jill and I proceeded to try to find the light switches by feeling our way along the walls. Suddenly, an apparition of even blacker appearance filled the doorway and a voice said, "Pshaw. What the devil's going on here?" It was our military man, Colonel Smitherman. Jill explained that we were merely making the rounds and had been unable to find the light switches; it was too dark for the good Colonel to see that we had been at least eight feet apart, but it was fairly obvious that his mind, working with typical military precision, had added two and two together and firmly and unshakeably come up with seventeen. The Colonel brusquely told us that *he* was doing the rounds, and so, like two chastened children, Jill and I retreated in, I must admit, some merriment, to the house and told Jill's mother about our adventure and the obvious and erroneous conclusion to which the Colonel had leapt. I confess, in all honesty, that the erroneousness of his conclusion was then, and has been ever since, a source of some regret to me.

There were at Applegarth two attractive and friendly dogs, Judy and Kim, and as dogs and I have always been on good terms, I soon became firm friends with these two and volunteered my services as official dog walker. The older daughter of the house, Pam, owned a horse, and as horses and I have always seemed to be a part of each other's lives, I offered to look after this animal when Pam was away and the horse was stabled.

The Stevens family extended to me every possible kindness and did much to raise my spirits from the mess of self-pity into which I had allowed myself to sink. I did my best in return to help them in such small ways as I could. However, my debt of gratitude remains outstanding.

Again, I did not fit in with my colleagues very well, for they came from social and environmental backgrounds very different from mine. Most were at Applegarth because they were either stupid or idle, but it was not an inexpensive school and most of the boys were also wealthy. I was not wealthy, nor was I stupid, and I was, in many ways, not idle. I did not preserve a "them and us" attitude towards teachers or the Stevens family and found the attitudes of many of my fellow-students appalling in their insensitivity and coarse brutality. On the other side of the coin, the warmth and friendship of Jill and her family more than cancelled out the disadvantages of the place, and I became almost as happy at Applegarth as I had been at Lapley Grange, and, after the purgatory of Magdalen, it was a joy to me to be able to enjoy the process of learning again. For the most part, the teachers at Applegarth were talented men who were interested in what they were doing, and again I began to take an active interest in learning.

Life at home at The Kilns was becoming filled again with the dark shadows of foreboding, for Jack was ill, Warnie was not at his best; his worry over Jack plagued him and on occasion he sought relief in neighbouring pubs; and the Millers' insidious campaign was proceeding apace. Then, at the time when both Jack and Warnie needed all the support and help that I could have offered them, blinded by my own self-pity and pursuing the fool's ends of a typical uncaring, callow youth concerned with no-one but myself, I deliberately and coldly withdrew my loyalty and my support from The Kilns and left myself only as a problem for Jack and Warnie to add to their worries.

CHAPTER 17

The Last Summer

IN THE GROUNDS of The Kilns there was a small two-room wooden cottage, very similar to the one in which Fred Paxford lived; it was away behind the greenhouse and looked out upon the masses of bright lupins which had taken over what had once been the tennis court. This cottage was, when I first arrived at The Kilns, empty and neglected, forgotten by all except for the shroud of creepers and ivy, which all but engulfed it. When I asked about this little building, I was told that it had been Mrs. Moore's house. I asked, "Do you mean Maureen's mother?" I was puzzled, for I had always understood that she had lived in The Kilns itself. "Oh, no, no, no. This was a different Mrs. Moore." I felt that the subject was closed and I enquired no further. I never did discover who or what this other Mrs. Moore was, or why she had a cottage in the grounds of The Kilns. However, there is probably some totally ordinary explanation; perhaps she was a bygone housekeeper or cook. Anyhow, for a while David had the use of "the Bungalow," as it was called, and when he no longer had any use for it, I took it over. It soon became a refuge and a place uniquely my own.

By this time, I had been given the gift of friendship by a group of very wonderful people. First, I met Freda. Freda Freeman was a very pretty brunette, with an innate sense of fun. I met her because while riding my bicycle one evening near the Risinghurst Community Centre, I managed to fall clean over the handlebars and onto the road. Picking myself up, I heard a peal of gay laughter and, looking around, I saw Freda running over to me. "Did you hurt yourself?" she called out, and then apologised for laughing. The whole of that area was lit by the orange glow of the sodium vapour lights which had been used on the new A40 (now M40) dual carriageway where it approached the Green Road Roundabout, and the rich orange light made Freda's natural prettiness take on a kind of faerie beauty. We became friends, who met in the street and stood and chatted and teased. Soon, I met Freda's sister, Jean, and Jean's boyfriend, Mike, and another boy, Terry. At first, I was much too shy to accept the oft-repeated invitations to come into the house and listen to records or whatever, but finally Jean got sick of my reluctance and one evening she firmly grabbed my arm and pulled me into the house.

Ken Freeman was a master plumber, and that was back in the days when the term "master" still meant something, before the advent of soft copper piping and even before the use of copper at all. Ken had served his apprenticeship and had learnt the skills of a trade which in that time was more an art than a mere trade. Water pipes in those days were made of lead, copper being kept almost entirely for gas, and to bend lead piping without kinking it involved the skillful use of strings of "bending bobbins" or a little later "bending springs." Joining lead pipes was an art form in itself, for the joints were "wiped," a process involving the use of a tallow-impregnated linen pad, a blowtorch and copious quantities of molten solder. The solder, while being kept hot and at just the right consistency by the judicious use of the blowlamp, was wiped around the juncture of the two pipes to be joined, as they also were heated, until the joint was a solid mixture of the metal from the two pipes and the solder, at which point the whole mass was allowed to cool. A well-wiped joint looked like a smooth swelling of the pipe and when the water was at full pressure allowed not one single drop of leakage. There were joints of various shapes and types for different purposes: some were relatively easy to make, like the "taff" joint, popular for joining waste pipes, for it was a quick and easy vertical joint, but would stand no pressure; others were diabolically difficult, and I most often wound up with a large heap of slumped lead/solder mixture on the floor when I attempted them. These days, plumbing is so easy that every farmer can manage it. Even I can plumb out a complete house with ease. But Ken Freeman was master of a difficult and demanding trade.

Ken's wife, Jean Freeman, was a kind and caring lady. She worked several days a week as a domestic help for a widow who lived in Headington and spent the rest of her time looking after her three daughters. When I joined this family circle, the eldest daughter, Ann, had already left home, and Jean and Freda were still at school. Terry had just joined Ken as an apprentice plumber. Mike also joined them when he left school. Jean, Freda, Mike, Terry and I soon became a close-knit group. My affections soon changed from Freda to Jean and of course this caused some tensions and difficulties. However, Jean was "going steady" (at the age of fifteen) with Mike, and I never managed to change that situation, try as I might. We had our occasional fights and hurts, but on the whole we all got on extremely well together. Looking back I can see that I must have been something more than a nuisance to those two understanding and compassionate parents. They obviously knew very well what the slow disintegration of my family structure had done and was doing to me, and they took me into their environment with a warmth and sympathy which I have never forgotten. I went back to England on fleeting visits four times after I left in 1967, and each time I tried to locate these good people but was unable to do so. (I finally was successful in 1984.) I am aware of just how much they did for me, and my feeling for them is still as strong as it was before we all drifted apart. Jean, Freda, Mike, Terry and I—"the Gang."

I cleaned out the bungalow, furnished it with odd bits and pieces, rented one of the two rooms out to Ken Freeman as a workshop-cum-store-room, and the other became "the Gang Hut." There we would meet to talk, play records and hold parties. For quite some time, I used it as a bedroom also, and spent as little time as I could in The Kilns. The Kilns was again filled with sadness and despair and, in addition, there was now also a murky sense of evil there. I felt and recognised the feeling of eventide; I felt but did not understand the presence of evil and so, instinctively, like Fred Paxford, I began to withdraw from the household, spending as much time away from it as I could. I spent my time at the Freemans' house, out in the streets, alone in the wood, or over in my refuge reading or in company with my friends. I rode a motorbike by this time and I was at home as little as I could manage. I left Jack to his misery and his fears about Warnie's alcohol problem. I left Warnie to his worries about Jack's decline in health. In cowardice and self-pity, I deserted the home and the two men whose company and loving support had for so long been all that had preserved my sanity. When at home from school, I was rarely at home. I know now that I could have done far more than I did to help both Jack and Warnie to bear the burdens which were their lot, but with the blind selfishness which is characteristic of egocentric teen-aged boys, I was too wrapped up in myself to spare time for others.

Strangely, Jack and I had, through these difficult years, become very close, and I think that he understood quite well the reasons for my reluctance to be a part of The Kilns at that time. At first, after Mother's death, with almost unbelievably naïve complacency, I never doubted that The Kilns and Jack would always be there for as long as I needed them. Then, when it began to dawn on me that there was an increasing likelihood of Jack being snatched away, and with him The Kilns, I reacted by rejecting The Kilns entirely and by not daring to love Jack any more than I already irrevocably did. Once, when in discussion with Jean Wakeman I said, "Well, if Jack dies, then what?" Jean had replied, "If anything happens to Jack, you'll come and live with me, and that's that!"

Jean visited The Kilns to see me, she entertained me with hilarious tales of her work, she arranged holidays for me and she generally showed herself to have been a true friend of my mother's. She became a friend of mine. To the Freeman family, to Jean Wakeman and to the Stevens family I owe my life, for without these people I almost certainly would have ended it in 1962. I was not suicidal in the usually accepted sense of the word; I did not actually desire death or even the cessation of life, but I simply could not see any point in life, for it had become so empty and the future, it seemed, was likely to be empty also. My friends' gifts of warmth and love began to give life some colour again, and I began to look around me again instead of only inside myself. By the summer of 1963 I was living at relative peace with the world.

I was excited about the summer holidays that year, for Jack was planning a trip for both him and me to Ireland; he would visit his friends and relations, whom he wanted me to meet, and I would explore the hills and valleys of Eire and would also act as porter and assistant to Jack, for he could no longer manage his own bags and travel arrangements. To me, the thought of being away from the oppressive atmosphere of The Kilns and yet with Jack was a combination devoutly to be wished, and visiting Ireland, of which I had heard so much, was an exciting prospect in itself. We were to travel by ship, sailing on Monday the 12th of August, and were to spend time in both Eire and Northern Ireland. Hotels were booked, as also were the berths on the ferry. On the 15th of July, Jack had a heart attack and the trip had to be cancelled. Warnie, unable to face Jack's deteriorating condition, fled to the mists of Ireland and the fog of alcohol about the end of May and did not return until September.

I went to the Acland to visit Jack, and we chatted for a while. Suddenly Jack asked me what time it was, and when I told him he said, "Well, hadn't you better be getting along down to the station then?" "What for?" I asked. "To pick up the au pair girl. Didn't Mrs. Miller tell you? She's coming in from Paris, and you're to meet her and take her up to The Kilns." This was said absolutely matter-of-factly, and sounded so plausible that I at once accepted it. "I had better call a taxi." I went off to the Hospital office, and telephoned for a cab, and almost before I had time to hang up the receiver the car was at the front door.

I went out and addressed the driver, a tall well-featured lady whose looks were marred by a hardness of expression, and asked her to wait whilst I went to get the money for the fare. I went back to Jack's room. "I'll need some money to pay for the taxi, Jack," I said. "What taxi?" was Jack's reply. "The taxi to go and fetch the au pair girl." "What au pair girl? Whatever are you talking about, Doug?" Jack stared at me as bewildered as I was. "Jack, a few minutes ago you told me that I had to go to the railway station to fetch a French au pair who is coming to help Mrs. Miller at The Kilns." Jack looked at me and began to smile. "It must have been a complete hallucination, Doug. I'm terribly sorry." Then he laughed and said that his mind was all that he had left and now that was going, too, and he laughed again. I did not find the situation at all amusing, until after I had borrowed the money from the Matron to pay the taxi to go away. Then on returning to Jack's room I began to see the funny side of it, but I don't really think that Jack and I were laughing at the same thing.

As I left the Acland that day, a familiar figure approached me. "I don't know if you remember me," he said extending his hand. "I'm Ronald Tolkien." I assured him that I did remember him, and we talked awkwardly for a few minutes. He was on his way in to visit Jack, and before we parted, he said, "If I can ever be of any help to you, if you ever need a place to stay, please don't hesitate to let me know." I thanked him, and he went in to see Jack, and I wandered away, my head full of fog and my heart full of pain.

The summer of 1963 was not as bad as might have been expected. Jack made light of his illness; I was engrossed in my own affairs and I didn't really want to perceive the approaching inevitability. There were other things to think about.

For a few weeks in that summer of 1963, our home was repeatedly visited by a clean-cut young man from North Carolina, U.S.A. He was a fan of Jack's and had written to say that he was planning to write a book about Jack and his writings. He was coming to England for his summer vacation and wanted to come to see Jack to talk. Characteristically, Jack advised him against the writing of a book about himself, but, of course, he invited the young man to visit.Walter Hooper arrived in England in June and came to see Jack at The Kilns. I liked him at once. He was a handsome young man about fourteen years older than I, and he had a charming and gentle manner about him. He seemed at first to be almost in awe of Jack, and this I found slightly amusing, but, nonetheless, charming. He soon became popular with the whole household and his visits were looked forward to by all of us. Walter Hooper quickly took in the strange and difficult situation that existed at The Kilns and he tried to assist in every possible way. Jack, at first, found his open enthusiasm (so much an American trait) something of an irritation and found that Walter's constant questions and discussions tired him, for Jack was a very sick man. However, he respected Walter's thirst for knowledge and spent considerable time with him. Walter, in his reverence for Jack and his work, wanted desperately to know as much as he could find out about his hero before he had to return to his job (he was, at the time, teaching at the University of Kentucky). With Warnie away in Ireland, presumably drinking himself silly, Jack was finding it difficult to handle his huge burden of letter-writing, and Walter offered to assist as best he could with this job, and for a short time was able to lift the trivial and non-confidential correspondence from Jack's shoulders.

Walter also offered to help with one other job which was now beyond Jack's physical ability. By this time, Jack had realised that he would never again be fit enough to resume his position at Magdalene and so resigned from his Chair at that College. Walter and I were despatched to Cambridge armed with lists of instructions. Walter had volunteered to take on the Herculean labour of sorting all the books and papers which Jack had accumulated in his Cambridge years. I went along to provide extra muscle power. We stayed there for a week, ensconced at the Blue Boar. We sorted books for days; I carried box after box of bound volumes to wherever Walter indicated. Walter, list in hand, laboured on, checking, packing, sorting and generally organising under a steadily increasing cloud of very learned dust. There were several days when Walter told me that as he only had papers to sort, he wouldn't be needing me, and I escaped to the river, where I hired a canoe and paddled up and down. Walter worked on in solitude, wading through the masses of handwritten pages with which Jack had filled his desk over the years. He probably had his job made the easier by the absence of my continual chatter, for having spent much of my time alone, I had developed into an incessant talker. Eventually, Walter and I had packed and despatched day by day to unknown (to me, anyway) destinations all the bits and pieces, the books and the papers, all that had remained of Jack's presence, in those rooms. They seemed stark and lonely without all Jack's clutter, and I felt for them; for as Walter and I left, I had the strange feeling that those rooms would miss Jack now that he was gone.

Walter had to leave England towards the end of August and return to the States, but he was to return to England after settling his affairs in America. Jack told me that now that Warnie had become unreliable, Walter was going to help as "a sort of secretary"! I didn't ask Jack how he was going to explain this to Warnie! However, it was not to be. A greater power than that of men had other plans.

CHAPTER 18

❧

Again the Hammer Falls

IT WAS RAINING; one of those dark, despondently wet and cold days of England's early winter, twenty years ago (to the very day, for I write this on the 22nd of November, 1983). I was at Applegarth; most of my studies there were completed, but there were still a few loose ends to tidy up. It was raining weakly and sporadically, as if no-one really cared one way or the other. I was inside doing much of nothing in particular when suddenly someone shouted, "They shot Kennedy!" My initial reaction was that of disbelief. Soon, time began to separate itself into longer and slower periods as more news came in on radio and television. Time passed hour by hour, then minute by minute, and the inescapable conclusion was forced upon us that it was true. A man with the potential for being one of America's greatest Presidents had met his death in a degrading and somehow typically American way. I felt deeply sorry for his wife and his family, for I knew what they must be feeling, and then I pushed such thoughts out of my mind and merely proceeded with the evening's routine. After supper I collected my books and set off wearily for the building in which I was to study.

Darkness falls early in England in November, and that night the dark was made blacker by the lowering cloud overhead, the musty smell of old leaves and my own depression. The path led from the back door, up three stone steps and on to the first of the outbuildings, a common room for the students. As I passed, I could see the flickering corpse-light of the television set as an announcer recounted once again the story of the Dallas motorcade and its disastrous end. I walked around this building and on past structures of indeterminate age from which bright yellow light fell onto the wet, black pathway and glittered there like lizards' eyes. These were study rooms, and each held a small number of students. At the end of the long, low building, the path (and I) turned left, and there, a further twenty paces or so on the right, was the room to which I was going. It was one of two relatively new buildings, well heated and lit. I entered the room and, with a lethargy born of boredom and a vague sadness which insistently hovered around the edges of my mind, I spread out my books, hooked a chair in beneath me and started to complete whatever task it was that I was assigned on that night. I don't remember what it was. I do know that I was unable to apply myself that evening. I had an uneasy sensation of waiting, although for what I did not know.

Time passed, perhaps an hour, and then the four or five of us in the room heard a sound that brought raised eyebrows and interested looks to the faces of my colleagues. The unmistakable sound of very definitely feminine feet, supported on high heels, *running* down the concrete path. (Perhaps I should add that Applegarth was an all-male school.) I looked up; I didn't know who was coming down the path so hurriedly, but I knew that she was coming for me, and I knew why. Pam, the somewhat glamorous elder daughter of the Stevens family, appeared at the door. "Don" (a nickname I have carried nearly all my life), "will you please come with me?" she said. Her voice was a brittle sound, nervous and worried. I began to gather my books.

"No, leave those," she said. "Just come." I looked at her, and Pam looked away. I felt the sympathy and pity for me that she was feeling. I knew that Jack was dead. I walked by her side back towards the house. "It's bad news, I'm afraid," she said, looking down at the path as it flowed backwards beneath our feet. "I know," I replied softly. "My stepfather has died, hasn't he?" "Yes, I'm afraid so." She did not look at me as we walked back to the house, for which I was grateful. At the top of the three stone steps we were met by Mrs. Stevens, who put her arms around me and again told me that Jack was dead. "I know," I said. "Pam told me." I looked up at the sky. The rain had started to fall again. I was glad of it, that my face would be wet with more than tears. Twelve days earlier, I had had my eighteenth birthday, and at eighteen a man is too old and not yet old enough to weep in public.

Pam had gone ahead into the house, and Mrs. Stevens and I followed. Jean Wakeman was waiting on the telephone, astounded that no-one had thought to tell me earlier. We arranged for her to come down to Surrey and collect me the following day. Warnie insisted on accompanying her; he was all but blind drunk and barely functional. Again I went back to The Kilns for a funeral.

No-one had thought to inform the American press of Jack's death, and I knew that Jack had a large following in the States, so I telephoned Walter Hooper, who was at home in America at the time. He was deeply saddened and promised to inform those whom he considered should be told in the States. I found that most of the arrangements for Jack's funeral had been made, but one or two things remained to be taken care of. I stayed at The Kilns for a few days. The telephone rang incessantly. I was tempted to leave it off the hook. I'm glad I didn't; some of the calls were important. " 'Ello, 'ello! Is 'at the Major's 'ome? Yer, well this is the Ampleforth Arms 'ere. We've got the Major, but 'e can't sort of walk, if yer know wot Oi mean. Can yer come an' get 'im? Yeah, we'll give yer an 'and ter get 'im inter the cab. Yeah, O.K. then, we'll see yer in a few minits then"; or "Evenin', Guvnor, Checkers 'otel 'ere. The Major's 'ere an 'e's sorter 'ad one too many. Will yer come an' get 'im? Oh, good. Ta-ta then."

Several times I had to call taxis and drive out to one or another of the surrounding pubs. Often, Warnie could not even stand. I had to lift him into the cabs. The publicans helped me, and the drivers, for Warnie was heavy and, when drunk, either petulant or obliging, depending on some totally unrecognisable and equally unpredictable factor. Sometimes, he was aware enough to produce a handful of pound notes with which to pay the fare. Sometimes I had to ask the driver to return later for his money. Once or twice, I paid the fare out of what little money I had. Warnie's alcoholism had been a family secret for many years, and so I told no-one of these episodes. In fact, I have never told anyone of them until now. However, I think Jean must have realised something of what was happening, for she resolved to get me out of The Kilns as soon as it could be managed. Warnie was not able to go to Jack's funeral, and it was I, once again the soldier on parade, who led the mourners behind the coffin, out of the Church of the Holy Trinity and over to the grave. I remember little about that day; a strange, still, silent day. No breath of wind moved the candle flame of that solitary sentinel which stood upon Jack's coffin; even outside, the flame stood straight and still and glowed against the darkness that seemed to be all around me.

Jean, again, was my strength and support. Peter Bide offered me his home as a refuge had I the need of it, but, as

I told him, Jean was taking me in; she had promised both Mother and Jack.

Of those few days of sorrow, anxiety, loss and worry, little remains in my mind. I lived in a kind of self-imposed mental fog, through which a few memories still wander like little lost ghosts. Some furniture and some of my belongings had been moved; some I helped to move to my new home: Horton-cum-Studley, Oxfordshire.

One memory, a more substantial shadow than the rest, is my bidding a farewell to Fred Paxford. His heavy arm across my shoulders, Fred said, "Ah, yer jus' gotter carry on, son. Yer jus' gotter carry on." I had never imagined that Fred could cry.

CHAPTER 19

Carryin' On

AND SO to Horton-cum-Studley; Horton at the bottom of the hill and Studley at the top. A beautiful little village of smug, thatched cottages rejoicing in their own obvious longevity, a row of Elizabethan almshouses for the aged, and Studley Priory, a building which for me symbolises the best of English architecture. A Mr. and Mrs. Parke bought the Priory from Mr. Bawtry and made it into an excellent hotel. Their son, Jeremy, and I soon became friends. We had fun bouncing air-gun pellets off the bell that hung over the ancient roof of the Priory and occasionally a tile or two, when one or the other of us missed. Jeremy is much the same age as I and now runs the Priory himself.

A distance of a mere few miles separates Risinghurst (where all my old friends lived) and Studley, but my life was flowing along new courses and, slowly but surely, I made new friends and let myself slide further and further from those to whom I owed so much.

My new home itself was a towering building of red brick, three stories high, an example of perhaps the best of Victorian styles, with a dark and interesting cellar beneath, full of old dust and cobwebs and reeking of decades of damp and darkness. This house had been built for the Vicar of that parish originally, and when the parishes had been amalgamated so that one man could serve the needs of several, the house was no longer needed by the church, and so was let. Initially, the tenant was one Francis Jones, a noted motoring journalist. Francis, his wife, Elise, and Jean shared the house, and eventually I joined the family, and the house and the people in it took on a quite Dickensian aspect.

Francis Jones. It seems to have been my privilege throughout my life to have met and known some of the finest human beings who ever lived. Francis was one of them. He was a grand old man. Francis had learnt to fly during the First World War and had successfully flown repeated sorties in F.E.2s and Vickers Gun buses and the like through that conflict. He had, in the ensuing peace, become a motoring journalist and had, at the height of his career, employed Jean Wakeman as his secretary. Now, when I joined the household, the roles were all but reversed, for it was Jean who was the successful journalist, and Francis was growing old and tired. He still wrote, but more and more it was Jean's work which supported the household. Time had demanded its tax of Francis and age had taken its toll.

Francis Jones was, without doubt, one of the most terrifying drivers with whom I have ever ridden. He would place his right foot solidly on the accelerator pedal and wait, his left foot anchoring the clutch pedal firmly to the floor, the gear box selected to any handy forward gear, wherever Francis suspected that first *should* be. When he was satisfied by the agonised roar of the engine that the valves were about to bounce straight through the rocker cover, he would slide his left foot sideways off the pedal and allow the return springs to engage the clutch! Bellowing, bucking and leaping like an enraged bull, the car would rear up on its hind legs and hurl itself forwards (or occasionally, if Francis had erred, backwards); while Francis, his pipe clenched between his teeth, an expression of grim determination on his face, wrestled the steering wheel savagely from side to side, narrowly avoiding disaster at every swerve, his steady soft stream of mild imprecations accompanying the screams of tortured machinery and shrieking rubber.

Francis and I were both in the habit of going around to the Priory for a drink after dinner, a distance of perhaps a quarter of a mile, and I would try to plan my evening so that I would be on my way before Francis left, or busy until after he had gone, for Francis, dear old Francis, found it difficult to walk that far and if there was anything with wheels available, he would drive. Also, he would be sure to offer me a lift, which, unless I could come up with a good reason, I could not refuse, for I would not have hurt him for the world.

Once in a while, when I misjudged my timing, I had to accept and then experienced five minutes or so of sheer terror as we shot past other cars, their occupants white-faced with horror as we brushed paintwork, and then thrashed our way through the shrubbery up the drive of the Priory, where Francis would stand the car on its nose by the simple expedient of throwing his full weight onto the brake pedal. After a trip like that, I was quite often staggering in a worse fashion than Francis, who, like many elderly men, had that studied lurching gait which comes from a decaying sense of balance. Locals engaged in holding up the bar would say such things as "Drove around with Francis, did you? Well, then, you'd better start with a whisky tonight!" And I would lie in my teeth (I had to, to keep them from chattering) and say something like "I don't know what you all go on about. He drives very well, really." Of course, he had been an expert driver for many years; the skill was still there in his mind, but he was forced to adapt it to the demands of his ageing physique. I became very fond of this great old character, and I still am.

Francis had a mischievous sense of humour, too. He had been involved in the early development of aerial bombing. In those days, one hefted one's bomb with one hand (by a handle attached behind the fins) over the side of the cockpit, lined it up while controlling the aircraft with the other hand and, at the appropriate moment, let go! I found one of these bombs being used as a doorstop. "Francis," I said, "is this thing live?" "What? Eh? Oh! Ah! Well, I shouldn't wonder. No, I shouldn't wonder at all," he muttered, and stomped off into the depths of the house somewhere, leaving me staring aghast at the ten or fifteen pounds of, to my mind, highly probable sudden death which I held in my hands. Last July, when I was telling my sons about this episode in Jean's presence, she insisted that it was a dummy, but I'm *still* not sure about the darn thing!

Jean had as a pet at that time (and for years afterwards) a pure-bred bulldog, Augustus (Caesar, no doubt), commonly known as "Gusto," for this was a quality which he possessed in great quantity. Often, Francis would drive through the village accompanied by Gusto sitting bolt upright on the passenger seat, observing the passing world with the steady, superior gaze of which the bulldog is master, well aware, as he invariably is, that he rules the world. Humourists among my friends often insisted that they had seen Gusto driving. On one memorable occasion when I was (happily) on my way into Oxford on my motorbike, I witnessed Francis (who was coming the other way) take a double right-angle bend, a right followed by a left, so hard that he rolled a tyre completely off the rim and let all the air out. The small foreign car he was driving disappeared momentarily under a shower of small stones, as it hurtled into a 360° spin and came to rest beside the road, leaving Francis sitting disconsolately at the wheel of the still rocking machine, watching the gravel which still pattered down all around. Awestruck, I pulled up to see if I could help and changed the wheel while Francis stomped about charging and trying to light his evil old pipe, all the while muttering about the damn-fool cars they build these days.

Francis was indeed a fine man. He had established himself as a hero in the First World War and he had lived out the rest of his life in the same hero's mould. He is gone now, too, but I will never forget him, even though I knew him for only a few short years.

Elise Jones was a different type of person altogether; frustrations and resentments had gradually embittered her over the years. She possessed a sharp, sometimes malicious tongue and a monumental tactlessness which I have never seen equalled. A grim expression was her habitual cast of countenance; her old face had taken on, it seemed, an almost permanent mould of disapproval, but when she smiled her whole face lit up and her eyes twinkled like two bright stars on a frosty night. It was only a pity that she did it so seldom. It was difficult to win a smile from Elise, but when you did, it was well worth the effort. I won't pretend that I really liked her, but then, I never really disliked her, either. I found her at times irritating and petty, at times malicious and hurtful and at times utterly charming and enchanting.

Jean and I had been friends for a long time and knew each other well. Jean had bought the house some time earlier, and thus she was really the Chatelaine of the Castle (this, I think, was the cause of some animosity on Elise's part). We had our arguments and disagreements, over my conduct chiefly, but on the whole we all got on together surprisingly well.

My first arrival in Studley was marked by two events which stand out in memory, one far more important than the other. The first, a trivial thing, but heart-warming, was that as Jean and I drove ceremoniously into the drive, we both burst into gales of laughter, for Elise, bless her, had hung from the upstairs windows both the British Union Jack and the American Old Glory by way of a welcome gesture. The second, which set my heart on fire, was that I met Sue.

Susannah lived with her mother in a lovely little place with the name "Windflower House." Probably out of charity and most likely at Jean's request, Sue and her mother decided to invite this unfortunate newcomer to the village, this poor waif that was me, to attend a party that they were giving for Sue's friends. I didn't really want to go to a party; in fact, I really *didn't* want to go to a party. I would far rather have just withdrawn into my shell like a hermit crab and sealed the door behind me, and I think Jean could see the danger of my doing just that. Anyhow, my dissembling was in vain, for Jean was adamant that I should go, and anyone who knows Jean will know that when Jean is being adamant, one might as well dispute the tide-right on the sands at Mont St. Michel. I went.

Dutifully, I walked past the Priory gate and down the short, steep drive to Windflower House, feeling nervous, awkward and embarrassed, and with no illusions concerning the reasons for which I had been invited to this gathering, the merry sounds of which I could just discern from within the house. I took a deep breath and thought, Well, might as well get on with it. And I reached out and pressed the doorbell. I waited at the door, feeling the frost close in around me and breathing the sweet smells of wood and coal smoke drifting on the cold night air. Nothing happened. Slightly amused and slightly irritated, I rang the bell again and waited. Suddenly, the door was flung open, and I, looking at my feet, which were unaccountably shuffling about almost of their own volition, mumbled in my embarrassment, "I'm . . . um . . . I'm Doug Gresham." The voice that answered me was filled with the music of life and as warm and gentle as a soft summer breeze, seeming to carry with it the scent of distant flowers. "Hello," it said. "I'm Sue; do come in." Astonished, I looked up, and there before my astounded eyes stood a stunningly beautiful girl. She had long dark hair, which fell about her shoulders, gleaming and shining in the light, her face was pale, setting off the red of her lips, and she possessed a perfectly delightful figure. She was wearing flat shoes, white ankle socks, a tartan skirt and a white knitted roll-necked jumper, which she filled quite adequately. When my gaze finally reached her huge brown eyes, however, I started to drown in them. Sue looked at me and I looked at Sue. I would have been quite content simply to stand there and stare until I froze into a solid block of ice, but she tilted her head to one side, laughingly reached out an arm and pulled me through the door. "Well, don't just stand there. Come in," she said. "It's cold out there."

I remember very little of anything about that party other than Sue. I watched her flit from person to person, from group to group, her eyes flashing with laughter and excitement. Sue and I very soon became friends, and more than friends. I was working at Roger and Pat Jones's farm, and Sue was studying, but we spent hours together day after day. I would hurry around to Sue's house in the evenings, and we would sit together and talk, or listen to music, or we would lie on a sofa, our arms around each other and simply relax, enjoying each other's company. We never made love; we never became lovers in a physical sense, but we were (and in a way still are) lovers in a purely emotional sense. Sue was the first woman, as opposed to girl, with whom I ever "fell in love." Sue and I developed a deep and enduring love for each other. Time and circumstance caused us to drift apart; Sue married Chris and I married Merrie. Gradually, we followed our different fates.

Having by now achieved the necessary O and A levels, I was qualified for an agricultural college in all but one way. I still had to perform at least twelve, and preferably eighteen, months' work on a farm or farms of general or mixed-farming type. I had already been working at every opportunity for a neighbour who ran a pig farm and, although I had gone there in fear and trembling, for it was the first time I had ever asked for a job, Roger and Pat Jones, who ran the farm, turned out to be wonderful people, and they taught me a great deal, not merely about farming, but about life in general, and about myself. Roger and Pat became great friends of mine. In order to widen my agricultural experience, Jean began to make enquiries about where I could go to learn more of the practical elements of farming.

I was sent (initially against my will) to a farm in Somerset, owned by Sir Edward Malet and run by himself, his wife and their son, Harry. I was to remain at their country estate for six months and there I was to begin a chapter of my life that was to bring a whole new dimension of both happiness and pain into my world, for it was at Chargot that I met and fell in love with a blonde, blue-gray-eyed niece of Sir Edward's who was, and is, utterly beautiful in body, mind and spirit. I soon made up my mind that sooner or later I would marry Merrie.

I went to Chargot a rebel; I objected to the whole idea behind Jean's delight in finding such an aristocratic environment for me. I had lived for years in an academic household, but had mixed, by my own choice, with people of the working class. Jean thought it was high time that I learnt more of the other end of the social scale. Of course, she was right, and the experience was invaluable, but at the beginning, I didn't like it. Thus, I first went to Chargot with considerable reluctance. In addition, I had become by this time a typically self-oriented, self-opinionated, boorish young fool. Much to my shame now, I had also realised the intrinsic value (false, of course) of being the victim of tragedy and I began to play upon it. Had it not been for the genuine Christian charity of Sir Edward and Lady Malet, I would probably have been sent home in disgrace within the first month. This particular illness, a sort of exploitive pride in self-pity, met its height and cure at Chargot. I developed the techniques of conversation-bending to a fine art, and within five or ten minutes I would drag, by brute force if necessary, the topic around to me and my terrible experiences and sad plight, and then bask in the light of sympathy. The Malet family tried to be understanding and accepted me to such a large degree that I didn't even suspect what an absolute idiot I was making of myself. Apart from my own foolishness, there was much to delight at Chargot, for Somerset is at once beautiful and wild, and Chargot is right in the middle of country long ruled by brigandry. Exmoor—a haunted, haunting land of great beauty and yet wild and grim to this day, but barely tamed to the will of man. I rode around the farm once a day, either on a horse or on a tractor, to check the stock and fences, and soon came to love the countryside, the village of Luxborough and the peculiar pinkness of that part of the world; the soil is pink, and even the concrete is pink.

Slowly, I settled into the environment of Chargot and complacently set out to do as little as I could get away with. I will, in my own defence, say that I was, at that time, actually afraid of being alone. If I was sent off by myself to perform some task or other, the chances were that I would leave the job half done and fly back to the house in search of human company. If I was alone, I started to think, and I did not want to think. A sore trial I must have been to those good people in those first few weeks at Chargot.

However, this situation was to be changed with the subtlety and suddenness of a sledge hammer. One morning, Lady Malet was reading her mail and she remarked, "Ah, Meredith is coming to stay and she's bringing a little friend." To Lady Malet, everyone was "little"; it was an adjective which she applied by habit to everyone and everything from the "little" man at the Post Office to "Ned's little horse" (a mare large enough to carry Henry the Eighth in full battle armour). Harry, on hearing the news, turned to me and said, "You'll like Merrie, Rabbit. She's the biggest flirt in the world." Perhaps I should explain that I was one of a succession of agricultural students to stay at Chargot; we were known by the generic term "farm rabbits" and frequently addressed simply as "Rabbit." Hasi, for that was his nickname, went on to say more about his cousin from Australia, but I'm sure that were I to quote him here, he would never forgive me, and I *know* Merrie wouldn't.

Hasi and I, it was arranged, would drive into Taunton in Sir Edward's beautiful Riley Pathfinder, a car which had been specially adapted to cater for both Sir Edward and Hasi's unusual tallness, for they were well in excess of six feet. The Riley was a lovely car, and Hasi and I set out in high spirits. By this stage, I had already found a young lady of considerable attraction and of (as it happened) good family who lived at Minehead, and she drove over to see me every so often, and I caught the bus to Minehead once in a while. I had met her at a Tupperware party to which Hasi and I had somehow been invited. The things I remember about that party are a fairly clear lead to my interests at the time. One: there was plenty of booze (important to an eighteen-year-old). Two: Hasi spent most of the evening with a very beautiful and charming young lady. Three: Anne. And four: we drove home in the "Trojan," an ex-Brooke-Bond tea van, diesel-powered but doorless, and it was snowing. If both Hasi and I had not been feeling on top of the world after the party, we probably would have frozen solid. The reason that I mention this young lady in this context is that I still feel guilty about what happened next, for after that trip to Taunton, I don't think I ever saw or spoke to Anne again. Let me explain.

Hasi and I drove into Taunton and, after conducting a few errands of farm business, proceeded to the railway station to meet the two girls. The train clattered and roared its noisy and noisome way into the station and soon I was being introduced to Merrie and Yogi. Yogi was (and is) a delightful and charming girl, full of enthusiasm and chatter. Merrie glanced at me just once and then ignored me, but in that one glance, she easily and permanently melted her way through the hitherto almost impregnable emotional armour with which I had surrounded myself. My dear Sue had, till then, been the only person to penetrate that shell. We all climbed into the Riley, Yogi and I in the back seat and Merrie flirting outrageously with Hasi in the front. We were back at Chargot for lunch, and that afternoon I was to go around the stock as usual. Politely, I asked if either of the girls would like to come; in all honesty, I must admit that I was both pleased when Merrie said yes and then displeased when Yogi also decided to come, for after knowing her for a mere hour or so, I already wanted Merrie all to myself.

Merrie and Yogi scampered away to change into farm-type clothes and I went to start the tractor. As we trundled around the hills and valleys, inspecting first one flock of

Devon-close-wool sheep and then another, checking the Red Devon cattle and then up the hills to look at the Scotch half-bred sheep, the two girls kept up a constant stream of fun-filled chat, gaily sprinkled with sparkling laughter. When we were up in one of the high fields known as "Leatherbarrow," after the tomb of some ancient warlord whose burial mound is still there, Merrie disclosed a burning desire to drive the tractor, a Fordson Dexta. She assured me that she knew all about tractors (untrue), having been brought up on a farm in Tasmania (true) and, thus deceived, I eventually allowed myself to be persuaded. After all, I thought to myself, Leatherbarrow is a big field and if I start her off in the middle of it, she really can't do much damage. Hah! It is only fair to say that both Merrie and Yogi have their own versions, both different, of what happened next and why, but if they want to have their say, they can write their own books; this is my book, and this is my version. Suffice it to say that Merrie blames Yogi, Yogi blames Merrie and, with feminine solidarity, they both agree that it was really my fault for being foolish enough to let Merrie drive in the first place.

In any case, Merrie was getting on famously, bouncing across the field, flat out in top gear, while I balanced with insouciant skill (I thought) on the foot plate, leaning nonchalantly against the mudguard and making small talk at the top of my voice to overcome the roar of the diesel engine. Suddenly, and with absolutely no warning, Merrie stood on both the clutch and brake pedals, and the tractor stopped dead; however, inertia being what it is, I did not. I sailed gracefully through the air at approximately the same speed as the tractor had been moving a mere second before. Then, gravity being what it is, I descended to earth to land ignominiously in a heap in front of the still roaring tractor. Ruefully, I picked myself up and brushed the dirt and sheep droppings from my clothes. Merrie, on seeing that I was unhurt, sat down again in the tractor seat and calmly and unthinkingly took her feet off the pedals. Bellowing, the little blue tractor reared up on its back wheels and hurled itself at me! Again I flew through the air, this time, at least, self-propelled, as with a mild protest, something like "Yaaahgh!" I flung myself to one side. As I sprawled again on the sweet-smelling turf, spiced liberally with evidence of the good health of Sir Edward's stock, the tractor roared past me and away into the distance, leaving behind both me and a torrent of Merrie's beautiful, uninhibited laughter as, in fits of giggles which bounced around on the wind like soap bubbles, she brought the tractor around in a wide sweeping circle and stopped to collect what was left of me.

I decided as I climbed back into the tractor seat that this was the woman I wished to marry and spend my life with, that this was the woman whom I wanted to be the mother of my children. By the grace of God, she is. That day saw the beginning of part two of my life and the beginning of the end of part one. I began to enjoy being at Chargot in spite of myself. Somerset is breathtakingly beautiful country, similar in some ways to Wales, with its lovely rolling hills, steeply cut here and there, with fast-flowing streams, and dotted with copses and small patches of forest. There are ancient ghosts in Exmoor, too, that flit and twitter in the night skies of fields such as Leatherbarrow, where the burial mounds of centuries-dead chieftains still rise with an air of threat from the otherwise flat hilltop. Mists rise sadly from the trees of the valley-floor forest lands, and local legend has it that these are smokes from the ghost fires of charcoal burners who worked these forests in the dark ages.

It was in this setting, the country of Lorna Doone, that I first realised that I was a fool, and a conceited fool into the bargain. I was told so, in no uncertain terms, by that same Merrie whom I adored. She watched as I left tasks incomplete, steered all conversational topics around to myself and generally behaved in a bumptious, braggart and idle manner. Merrie watched the eyebrows raised and Lady Malet's expressive shrug of the shoulders, which all too clearly said, "What can you do with this child?" For child I was. One night when Merrie and I still sat, alone before the fire in the hall, Merrie with a purpose in mind, and I because I wished nothing better in life than simply to sit and stare at her, after everyone else had gone to bed, Merrie quite simply and straightforwardly told me how I was destroying myself and how I was by my obnoxious behaviour becoming less and less liked in the household and less and less trusted on the farm. She cut no corners and pulled no punches. My reactions passed through being indignant and defensive (I was told to shut up and listen) to being hurt and astonished that I had been so misunderstood (I was told to shut up and pay attention), on to the sickening realisation that Merrie was telling, brutally and honestly, the truth. She made me sit and listen without interruption until, when I finally began to feel utter despair, I was told how to set to and correct the situation. Having at last accepted that I had been behaving both badly and foolishly, I could see that, as a farm rabbit, I had, to date, been a dead loss!

The next day, when sent to put some grain through a hammer mill and some through a roller for stock feed, I worked until the sweat ran stinging into my eyes and I had filled every bag available, instead of following my customary practise of doing as little as I thought I could get away with. I spent the whole day in that dusty shed, despite the fact that I ached to be with Merrie. I only stopped when I ran out of sacks.

I can't say that I was cured, for I wasn't, and I had many relapses, but I was at last pointed in the right direction. When their holidays came to an end, Merrie and Yogi returned to London and St. Thomas' Hospital, where they were both nursing. I missed Yogi for her cheerfulness and humour, but Merrie when she went took away the very light of the sun. Lady Malet had noted my reaction to Merrie's presence (and indeed so had everyone else), for when Merrie left, she turned to me and said, "Don't worry, my Rabbit; she'll soon be back." She was, but before then, I had taken matters into my own hands. I asked for, and was granted, a short leave of absence. Merrie had given me her London address and said casually that if I were ever in London, I should look her up. Leaving Chargot, I headed straight for London and soon found my way to 86 St. Georges Square, Pimlico. Nervously, I rang the doorbell. Somewhat to my surprise, I was made very welcome and was invited to stay. There was a spare bedroom of sorts behind the kitchen at the back of the flat, almost big enough for a pantry. It was filled with a narrow single bed and assorted suitcases and junk. This small room and indeed the flat itself were to become almost a second home for me over the next few years.

Four girls at a time shared this habitation, in order to keep costs down to a bare minimum. It was the ground floor of what had once been a fairly elegant though small town house. Merrie, Yogi, Erica or "Eckie" and Fiona were the inhabitants at that time, but names and faces changed quite frequently over the next few years. Merrie and Yogi were the only two who remained there for all the time that I knew the place. However, let it be said that in all the time that I visited the flat, there was only one girl that I did not like who ever lived there, and I became very fond of several of them. Yogi and Eckie are still friends of ours. Fiona was very kind to me in those early days, for when she saw how miserable I was whenever Merrie was out at work or with one of her legion of admirers, Fiona engaged me in long conversations which kept my mind bouncing and busy.

My first visit to 86 St. Georges Square was interrupted, because Jean, who had no idea that I was not at Chargot, had telephoned, and Lady Malet, who had, up until then assumed that I had gone to Studley, very quickly added two and two together and rang the flat to suggest that I ring Jean to tell her that I was all right and that I would soon be returning to Chargot. This I duly did, but I did steal an extra day or so. The bed in that back bedroom had a mattress which felt as if it were stuffed with old tank traps and truck chassis (the girls all shared one larger bedroom at the other end of the flat) but to be kissed good night by Merrie I could have slept on broken glass, and slept well. That first trip to London did two things. First, it introduced me to the idea that I could formulate a plan of action completely independently of any advice or consultation with anyone, and then carry it out. Second, it gave me my first glimpse of the standard of Merrie's male friends, or, in other words, I had made a sortie into no man's land and appraised the enemy. Frankly, my chances looked pretty grim. The specimens I met on that and subsequent visits were all older than Merrie (she is nearly two years older than I) and were men of means, already embarked upon professional careers such as law or medicine. I was penniless, young and without visible prospects. The best I could hope for was a job managing someone else's farm. In my favour, there were only two possible advantages. First, Merrie loved animals, the country and outdoor life; second and most important, though I did not recognise it at the time, Merrie had experienced a shattering childhood (far worse, in some ways, than my own) at the hands of inept and foolish parents and had a need to be loved, not merely desired for her looks (she is stunningly beautiful), but loved utterly and completely, and that I could handle. On one visit to her flat, I found her absolutely despondent. She had received a letter from Australia telling her that the boy-friend she had left behind there, who had promised to wait for her (she was supposedly on a six-month working holiday), had married another girl. She felt at once ne-glected and betrayed. My reaction was in two parts, for, while I was deeply grateful to this antipodean fool for kindly removing himself from the competition, I would cheerfully have achieved the same result by throttling him for the pain he caused Merrie.

That night, in the kitchen of that dingy, but much beloved, flat, strangely like Avoca House, I, in fear and trembling, asked Merrie to marry me. She laughed and cried at the same time and she kissed me softly and carefully, but she did not answer my question. I went back to Chargot.

After six months, during which I saw Merrie on several occasions when she visited Chargot, my allotted time there came to an end, and I left, not perhaps fully cured, but certainly a very different person to the gauche, conceited, self-centred idiot I had been such a short while earlier. With feelings of great regret, I left Chargot. I had been reluctant to go there in the first place, and now I was reluctant to leave. I spent several holidays back at Chargot in the years which followed and I was always made welcome.

From Chargot, I went to a large intensive mixed farm a mere fifteen miles or so from Studley, Glympton Park Estate. I saw Warnie occasionally while I was there, but I still shied away from his loneliness. My chief concern was saving money, for now I was being paid a wage, instead of pocket money. At Glympton I learnt a great deal about the actual mechanics of farming and I learnt to work till tears of pain mingled with sweat on my face. The manager of Glympton at that time was John Dixon. Once, a gang of men, including me, was loading fifty-six-pound bags of potatoes onto a truck. We passed them from man to man from the heap in the shed to the truck. John Dixon arrived and, placing me at number one, or, in other words, as the poor bunny who has to pick up the sacks off the heap, he took the number-two position. I picked up a bag of spuds and passed it to him and reached back and grabbed another. When I turned around, he was waiting for me with a grin on his face. "Come on, lad. Hurry up," he said. No matter how fast I worked, every time I turned around there he was with that grin. Faster and faster I lunged for those bags of potatoes; faster and faster I hurled them back to John and they just tumbled back along the human chain like rats falling down a drainpipe. My heartbeat was roaring in my ears and every muscle in my body was screaming for rest, but John was still waiting there with that grin. Finally, someone outside the shed sang out "Truck load!" I slowly and carefully stood up, unbending my back very gently. John Dixon paid me his highest accolade. "Aye, you'll do, lad," he said. He had not worked up even the faintest sheen of perspiration. We loaded the next truck a great deal more slowly, for John had left us to it. Month after month went slowly past and I earned and saved my pay.

Merrie and Yogi had decided to tour Europe on a hitch-hiking, camping holiday. This I thought was sheer madness, although it was probably less dangerous then than it would be now. However, they were determined, and in due course off they went to travel around the Continent for several months. Merrie had promised she would write to me, and she did. Cards and letters poured in, about one a week, from all over Europe. I saw Sue once or twice. She was the only person whom I could tell how I felt about Merrie, and a few other friends in the Oxford area, but basically it was a long, cold, empty spring.

I worked on at Glympton and Merrie and Yogi happily grasshoppered around Europe. As the summer progressed, however, Merrie's funds began to get low and she decided that she could no longer afford stamps and so stopped writing. Consequently, her regular postcards stopped arriving and I started worrying. This silence went on and on and I grew more and more worried and finally all but frantic. I started to think. I contacted some friends and they contacted other friends, and slowly, step by step, I began to trace the path of these two cheerful wanderers across Europe. I tracked Yogi down to her home in The Hague, in Holland, but could get no clear lead on where Merrie was. A friend in a surprisingly high place had told me that the two had split up. As a last resort, I phoned Yogi at her home, and she told me that Merrie's ultimate destination had been her brother Stephen's house in Hamburg. Stephen was living there as an officer of the Australian Immigration Service. I could not obtain either his address or his phone number, being rather inexperienced at this kind of work, but I reasoned that the best place to try to find him would be in Hamburg itself. To this end, I simply caught a train to Dover, my time at Glympton by now being officially at an end, a boat to Calais and a train to Hamburg. The train to Hamburg was full of a large group of teen-aged boys returning to Germany after a Youth Hostel holiday in England. These lads, obviously as inexperienced at international travel as I was, had managed to leave England with pockets full of coinage. The only places that would accept silver along the way across Belgium and Germany were the frankfurter and beer stalls to be found on every station platform. Alone and lonely, I was cheered by the generosity of these fellows, who pressed upon me beer after beer in huge waxed cardboard steins, each holding about a litre of the pale, frothy, rich-tasting beverage and insisted that I eat half a dozen or more of the great fat sausages, served with handfuls of sauerkraut. They were the first German sausages I had ever tasted in Germany; they were superb! The more I ate (with obvious enjoyment), the more they pressed upon me, indicating in broken English and sign language that they had to dispose of their coins somehow and what better way was there than beer and sausage? Somewhere along the rails of the night, we all sang raucous songs in German, English and gibberish, and still further along we all eventually, replete and warmed by good beer, good food and good fellowship, passed out. I arrived in Hamburg almost as soon as I had fallen asleep, in the desperately early hours of the morning. I lugged my suitcase to the end of the platform and, deciding that it was far too early to attempt any enquiries, I wearily sat down on it to rest and to wait for the hands of the clock to strike a more reasonable pose. I had been, by this time, eighteen hours travelling, with only three or four minutes of sleep, and had consumed copious quantities of rich sausage and strong beer. Reflecting gratefully upon my good fortune, I fell asleep. The next item of interest to enter my notice was the toe of a very shiny black boot busily prodding me in the short ribs; the foot encased in this boot was attached to the long leg of a tall, saturnine Polizei officer. "Guten Morgen, mein herr," he said with a bare hint of a smile. "Schlafen hier verboten ist!" I looked around me in astonishment; the sun was high and the place thronged with the people dashing here and there. I had slept for several hours on a busy railway platform in the middle of the Hamburg Eisenbahnhof!

The time was about 8.30, so I trudged off· to find a phone-box and started to search the telephone directory. There, sure enough, nestled amongst all the very foreign-looking names, was one that was pure gold as far as I was concerned: S. M. Conan-Davies, and his address. I had no change and so decided not to phone him, but to go straight away to his home to see if I could catch him before he went out somewhere, for this was a Saturday morning. I hailed a taxi and during the trip I mentally rehearsed the story. I would be a friend of his sister Meredith, who "just happened to be passing through" Hamburg on my way to London, and so forth. Soon I was standing nervously outside the door of a neat suburban house, hoping that (a) someone would be home and (b) that whoever it was would speak English. I took a deep breath and gently pressed the doorbell. Bing! Bong! went the chime. Nothing. I paused to think and began to formulate a new plan of action. Suddenly, I heard the sound of feet pattering down a carpeted flight of stairs within the house. There was a short pause and then the door opened to reveal, to my absolute delight, of all people, Merrie!

Her hair was sopping wet and wrapped turban fashion in a towel, and she was wearing a blouse and skirt which looked as if they had been put on very hastily, and indeed they had, for I had surprised her in the shower, washing her hair. We have a figure of speech in Australia which best describes her expression when she saw who was standing on her brother's doorstep by now wearing a foolish grin. She looked for all the world like a "stunned mullet" and stood there staring at me; it was as if she simply could not fit my presence into the reality of her surroundings. Finally, she managed to collect her wits and invited me into the house, plying me with questions. What on earth was I doing in Hamburg? Why had I come? How had I found her? And so on. I replied that I was in Hamburg *to* find her and to take her back to England. I was there because I loved her and missed her and had been worried about her, particularly when she ceased to write, and I had found her by asking lots of people lots of questions and by using my intelligence. To say that Merrie was flabbergasted is probably an understatement. I doubt if I have ever seen a more satisfactory case of "flabbergastion" in my life. After a while, I became aware of something a little odd. Merrie and I were, with the exception of Merrie's baby nephew Michael, alone in the house. I asked Merrie how this extremely convenient state of affairs came about, and a rather amusing side to the situation soon became apparent. An expedition had been planned for that day to Lübeck, and Merrie had suggested that Stephen and his wife, Ursula, should go by themselves so that they could have a day off together, while Merrie stayed at home and took care of Michael. At first, they wouldn't hear of it, but Merrie insisted, explaining that she wanted to wash her hair. In the end, Stephen and Ursula allowed themselves to be persuaded and off they went. Our problem was how to convince them that the whole thing was not a "put-up job" and pre-planned? I don't think we did, and I doubt if even now Stephen and Ursula really believe that Merrie had no idea that I was coming.

We spent happy days in Hamburg. As soon as Stephen, Ursula and I had been introduced and somewhat halting explanations made, they invited me to stay with them for a while, and Merrie and I rowed around the Alster and wandered the city hand in hand, laughing in the parks and seeing the sights. Soon, we returned to England. Merrie went back to her flat and resumed her job with a private nursing agency, and I went off to agricultural college. During our stay in Hamburg, I had once again asked Merrie to marry me. She simply smiled and kissed me, but she didn't answer my question.

CHAPTER 20

Dawnlight and Darkness

IN ABOUT 1951 I had stayed at Cressida Farm, a dairy and mixed farm owned and run by a friend of my father's. I can't remember exactly where it was, but Henry Wheeler and his family made me very welcome, and I got to drive the truck in the hayfield, or at least to steer it in a straight line down the row of bales as the men threw them onto it; I steered the big green John Deere tractor, and watched the Ayrshire cows being milked; I was butted clear across the road by a bad-tempered ram who was a lot bigger than I was, and I decided then and there that I wanted to be a farmer. I never changed my mind, and all my time thereafter was spent waiting to become one. Agricultural studies seemed to be indicated, and so to college.

The college I had decided to attend was my own mistake and no-one else's. I found it to be far from London (meaning, of course, far from Merrie), far from ideal and far from educative. I began my studies there with an active interest at first, but soon realised that I was not learning to be a farmer, but was learning estate management and like pursuits; also, the training leaned far too heavily on agricultural theory and was designed mainly for those who wished to remain in England. I had no desire to study the various sciences which governed the reasoning behind the established agricultural practises of Britain; I found the lectures about as stimulating as a bowl of cold custard and the lecturers, with one or two notable exceptions, about as intelligent.

I very soon knew that this college was not a place where I should be and that it was a total waste of my time. Let me hasten to add that this by no means indicates that the college did not perform the function for which it was designed; it did. It turned out dozens of estate managers and similar types, who could write N.D.A. (National Diploma of Agriculture) after their names. The problem was that I did not want to know what they were trying to teach me. The fact is, I would be embarrassed to write N.D.A. after my name even if I had the right, which I don't. For all that, I have been farming in a greater or lesser way now for the better part of twenty years. As I said, I chose the college, and I chose badly.

One facet of my existence there which I did find difficult to accept and which wasn't my fault was that at the age of twenty I was a student whose weekly pocket money was ten shillings, or one dollar. Warnie was my paymaster and he thought that ten shillings should be enough. Most of the other lads there, and many of the girls, had their own cars, some M.G.s and even a Lotus or two. (I would have settled for a Morris Minor.) They dressed well and they lived well. I, on the other hand, looked like a refugee and felt like one. I asked around and found that the average weekly income of spending money was seventeen pounds, or thirty-four dollars per student! Warnie himself had found a similar experience all but intolerable when he had been at Malvern College, for his father had kept him in penury.

I saved every penny I could lay my hands on, and I scoured the countryside around the college for part-time work, but the college had been there long enough for its students to have gained a bad reputation, and I found few who would employ me. When I had managed to save a few pounds, I would hitch-hike to London. Hitch-hiking was not easy at that time in England; there had been too many killings. Thus, I would leave the college on Friday evening and often not arrive in London until sometime on Saturday, when, dead tired, I would stumble through the streets, unable to afford the tube-train or bus. Sometimes Merrie and I would go out to dinner, and usually she paid, but I much preferred to merely laze around and talk, for I would be exhausted and knew that on Sunday evening, or Monday if it were a Bank Holiday, I faced the task of the all-night trek back to college. Merrie found my state of perpetual fatigue exasperating and inexplicable, but then, I never told her of the realities involved in my trips to London to see her.

During my holidays, I worked at Roger and Pat Jones's pig farm and saved every last cent of my money. On one occasion, I had a particular aim in mind: Merrie's birthday. Merrie always made a point of remembering when any of her flatmates was having a birthday and would arrange a dinner party or some other form of festivity to celebrate the event. She also made sure that there was a cake and so on. I cannot remember who was sharing the flat with Merrie at the time of which I am writing, but I seem to recall that Yogi was away somewhere and there were two other girls in residence. I had saved what, for me, was a largish sum of money and persuaded Pat Jones to accompany me to a jeweller to buy a present for Merrie. My selection took a long time as one by one I rejected all Pat's suggestions and one after another the shopkeeper's ideas were turned down. Finally, I saw a beautiful marcasite brooch in the shape of a large four-leafed clover. "Doug," said Pat when I pointed it out, "you can't afford that!" It was exactly what I wanted, but Pat was right. By the time I had bought it and posted it, I was left with less than three pounds to my name. However, I knew that of all the things I had examined, that was the right one for this occasion, and off it went to Merrie, and off I went back to college. The next weekend, as soon as I had finished work, I dashed home, had a bath and dressed in my best suit. I set out for London, my last few shillings tucked away in my pocket.

October is a dank, chill month in England, and it was a grim, foggy evening with a cold, grudging rain drifting down from the frigid black sky. Under these conditions, hitch-hiking is particularly difficult, for the weather gives motorists a sense of oppression and doom, and they are far less ready to stop for a young man hunched up inside his raincoat than they would be on a bright, sunshiny morning. Luck was out to dinner that night, for I walked a large part of the way from college to London, some 200 miles. It seemed like I walked all the way. Anyway, it was well into the following afternoon, in fact, the day of Merrie's birth, when, chilled through to the very marrow of my bones and utterly exhausted, I found myself trudging into the top end of St. Georges Square. A bright flash of unexpected colour caught my eye. There beside the road a barrow-boy had set up his wheeled stall and was selling bright, beautiful carnations. His brazier full of hot, glowing coals I found even more attractive, for I was so cold that I had lost all feeling in both my hands and my feet. I walked over to the brazier and stood for a moment or two holding out my hands to the warmth. "Yeah, Guv?" asked the ageing barrow-boy. "How much are the flowers, sir?" I asked, knowing all too well that I had only two pounds and five shillings. "Five bob each, Guv. Four fer a pahnd or ten fer two quid." Flowers out of season, and flown in from some overseas greenhouse do not come cheap in London. He must have seen my face fall, for his hard-bitten look faded and for a moment he looked at me and I saw that he looked almost as tired as I was. "It's her birthday, and I haven't much money," I began, when he broke in. "Tell yer wot, Guv'nor," he said. "Give us two quid an' Oi'll let yer 'ave a full dozen," and then he added savagely, as if to excuse his generosity, "Too bleedin' cold ter stand aht 'ere all bleedin' die any'ow. Sooner Oi gets rid of 'em, the 'appier Oi'll be!" I thanked him and he selected a dozen blooms of various colours, paused, and then added another. "Jus' for luck," he muttered. (The date was the 13th.) Quickly and skilfully, he wrapped the flowers gently in white tissue paper, and I handed him my last two pound notes, leaving a mere five shillings for emergency money.

Dizzy with cold, exhaustion and hunger, for I had not eaten since lunch at college the previous day, I leaned against one of the black-painted pillars of the portico of No. 86, clutching my carnations and inhaling their heavy scent. Finally, I pulled myself together and rang the doorbell. I was let in by a young man friend of one of Merrie's current flatmates, who led me into the sitting room. Merrie was seated alone, her back to the door, in an armchair; she was so miserable that she did not even turn around to see who it was that had arrived at the flat. I had intended to surprise her, and that I did. I reached over the back of the chair, placed the flowers in her lap, and said, "Happy birthday, darling," and kissed her. Her reaction was to burst into a veritable flood of tears, accompanied by tearing, heartbroken sobs. I was completely mystified. I knelt at her feet and held her in my arms, asking again and again what was wrong. Merrie could only shake her head and sob the louder. The young man who had let me in had discreetly left the room, and at length I discovered that everyone, family, friends, relatives near and far, and acquaintances and flatmates, everyone had forgotten Merrie's birthday. My present had not yet arrived, despite the fact that I had posted it a week earlier. (I feared that it might have been lost or stolen in the mail, but it turned up the following Monday.) Finally, Merrie managed to control herself and she asked me to take her out somewhere. So, embarrassing though it was, I had to explain that I couldn't, because I had no money left. She knew that I had been working and saving all through the last holidays, and thus it dawned on her that I had spent far more than I should on her present, as yet still in transit. Then she asked how I had got the flowers, and I had to admit that they represented all that remained of my worldly riches. At this revelation, she began to cry again. I had to leave to return to college the next day, but by then the world could have turned to ice around me and I would not have felt cold, for the previous evening I had asked Merrie to marry me, and this time she had smiled and kissed me and said yes.

CHAPTER 21

❦

The Kilns, Warnie and Others

WHILST I was discovering life and the joys of living, Warnie was losing life, his will for it and any joys it may have once held for him. Alone at The Kilns and poor in spirit, he began to turn more frequently to drink to subdue the pain. Mr. and Mrs. Miller began to take care of him, but I confess that I have doubts about their motives for doing so. Perhaps they really could not see any reason why Warnie should not drink. I remember once or twice in my hearing one or the other saying, "Go on, Major, have another. It'll make you feel better." I was horrified, for I knew all too well where the "odd drink or two" would inevitably lead, but I had had enough of sickness and sorrow, and I confess I felt disgusted and afraid. There was an almost tangible feeling of evil in that house, and I visited Warnie less and less often. Occasionally, I would spend the night at The Kilns, but was always made to feel unwelcome by the Millers, who would greet me with some cutting remark such as "Wot are you doin' 'ere? You don't live 'ere no more, you know"! When I visited The Kilns, it was accepted that I never made use of the doorbell, for I had not done so for ten years. I would simply walk into the house and search out Warnie.

He was usually to be found in his study and never failed to make me welcome, drunk or sober.

On one of these visits, on a chilly evening, I saw the study light was on, and so went into the house and straight down to the study. Sure enough, there I found Warnie. He was drunk and had spilt a large quantity of spirits down the front of his clothes. As I entered the room, he was barely conscious but attempting to light a cigarette. Within a split second, the whole of his chest was a mass of flickering blue flames. I tried to crush them with my hands at first, but soon my hands were also on fire. Fortunately for both of us, a blanket was lying on the second armchair in the room, the twin of the one in which Warnie was sitting. I seized the blanket and with it I soon managed to smother the flames. My hands were burnt, but not badly, for the alcohol had evaporated as it burnt, and the cooling of the evaporation had protected my skin from the heat of the burning. Warnie suddenly woke up, completely uninjured, and was amused to find me suddenly standing before him, cursing and shaking my hands to cool them. "Hello, Doug, young feller-me-lad," he cried out. "Have a drink, eh? Siddown an' have a drink," he invited, and I did. I had been badly frightened, so I poured myself a tumblerful of Vat 69 and sank gratefully into the second armchair and nursed my drink as Warnie rambled on, drifting from one topic to another. When Warnie was drunk, he often pretended to be even drunker than he was, and would say the most obscene things in the hope of shocking his listener. I don't think he ever knew that the shocking thing was not what he said, but that *he* was saying it. I also had been to boarding school, however, and Warnie's lascivious descriptions and questions had not the slightest effect on me, other than a deep sadness that Warnie was in such a condition that he would spout such filth with evident relish. Eventually,

Warnie passed out completely, dropping his lighted cigarette in his lap and his bottle on the floor. I threw away his cigarette, took away all the matches that I could find in the room and moved two full bottles of Vat 69 away to the kitchen. Fairly sure that he would not wake before noon the following day, I left him. It was a long time before I visited him again. I was disgusted by his condition and his behaviour. Now I find that I am disgusted by the behaviour which I exhibited at the time, for I fled, I ran away, leaving alone a tired, bereaved old man whom I might have been able to help, simply because I had not the courage and could not spare the time from my own hedonistic pursuits, to show a little understanding and compassion.

Warnie's suffering, his pain and anger at fate or God for taking away Jack's happiness with Mother and then Jack himself was too much for me, and, while Warnie fought a valiant rear-guard action, I turned tail and ran. My shame and sorrow are still with me; my only excuse is that I was young.

Mr. and Mrs. Miller persuaded Warnie (with some justification) that The Kilns was too big for him alone, and so he let the house to a tenant and moved to 51 Ringwood Road. Perhaps the Millers saw possibilities in the moving process, for Warnie "gave" them many small but valuable things; many others simply vanished. In return, they made sure that Warnie was kept supplied with drink and they sobered and tidied him up for occasional visitors. Warnie was not, by any means, constantly intoxicated, but he seemed never to be completely sober either. In fact, I cannot remember ever seeing him completely sober after Jack's death. It may be that it just happened that my visits coincided with his worst times. It may also be that my visits, unannounced as they were, did not give the Miller regime time to sober him up. However it was, I didn't visit frequently, for the Millers made it quite plain that I wasn't wanted, and I never again met the charming, gentle old Warnie whom I had loved and respected. I am convinced that Mr. and Mrs. Miller, seeing the chance of considerable material gain to themselves, not to mention the third-hand kudos of being C. S. Lewis's brother's keepers, gradually and insidiously worked their way into his confidence and his trust. However, on the positive side, they certainly did much to alleviate his loneliness in those years. They took him for long drives (he bought the car), they took him on holidays (he paid the bills) and they provided for his everyday wants and needs (he provided the cash).

Walter Hooper had returned to England shortly after Jack's death and he spent some time with Warnie when Warnie was at his very worst. Walter tried to sober Warnie up and persuade him to give up drinking; the Millers took the opposite stance and helped him to stay drunk. Walter Hooper was soon frozen out by the Millers.

Once, I took Merrie to visit Warnie, but Warnie was not fit to be seen and he was not fit to be heard. I was deeply ashamed and embarrassed; that was really the end of any direct relationship between us.

CHAPTER 22

Starting the Future

PLANS are easy to make and sometimes, if God takes a hand, they become easy to carry out. Merrie and I had a host of plans. First, I had to get myself out of that college as soon as I reached the age of majority—in those days, it was twenty-one years. Then we would marry and emigrate to Tasmania. I had discoverred that I was not quite penniless after all; my grandmother had left me a sum of money just about sufficient to use as a deposit on a small farm, at the prices of the day, in Australia.

I returned to college, lighter in heart and rich in happiness at the thought of all the great adventures upon which I was about to embark. Our year-long engagement was not without its traumas and problems. Once, we even broke it off, or, to be more accurate, Merrie broke it off. I was desolate and fled to Chargot. For the first time in three years, I did not tell Merrie where I was going and I did not contact her. I worked on the farm for a few days, driving my body to exhaustion and trying not to think about the future. Lady Malet knew exactly what was wrong and said exactly the right thing, which was nothing. Then one evening after I had been there for about a week, she came into the hall to tell me that I was wanted on the telephone. Her beautiful face was lit by a warm smile full of wisdom and pleasure. "But no-one knows I'm here," I protested.

"Oh, Rabbit, don't be silly," she replied. "Go and talk to Meredith!" Merrie had found that, grim though the prospect of life with me might be, she preferred that to the prospect of life without me. Instinctively, she had turned (as I also had) to Lady Malet for help and advice, and also she thought that Chargot was the most likely bolt-hole for me. Advice was something that neither of us lacked at that time; some of Merrie's relatives told me that Merrie was not good enough for me (!), some told Merrie that I was not good enough for her (?) and almost all my friends decided that Merrie was too good for me, but if she wanted to marry me, then I should grab her before she came to her senses! Some exceptions: Sue thought Merrie was ideal for me and I for her, and Jean also approved of our marriage, despite one or two fights along the way with both Merrie and me. Sir Edward and Lady Malet also wished us well, and Merrie's cousin Jonathon agreed to be the best man. Merrie and I were to be married in the Lady Chapel of Westminster Cathedral, for Merrie at that time was a Roman Catholic.

I had to take lessons in the teachings of the Roman church, and thus met Monsignor Anglim, a kindly and wise priest. I promised that our children would be baptised into the Roman Catholic Church. This promise I have kept and I will not inflict upon them any divisionary views, for I believe that sectarianism is one of Screwtape's most effective weapons against Christianity. The children know that I believe in God and in Jesus Christ, His son, and in the Holy Spirit and they know why. Their decisions about their involvement with things Christian will be of their own making as they develop their ideas and knowledge. I will guide them to the best of my ability and Merrie will do the same.

I went with my fiancée to Australia House in The

Strand to apply for an assisted passage to Australia. We were interviewed, examined, x-rayed and told that we would be informed whether we were considered suitable material for immigration or not by a collection of vaguely Cockney-sounding people who smiled a lot and usually greeted one with "Gooday!" although most of them were actually native employees. We learnt that we had been judged sufficiently whatever, and were to be accepted as assisted migrants. We were also told that because we had elected to travel by sea (a four-week cruise for ten quid? Why not?), there would be a wait of several months before we could obtain a berth. So we made leisurely plans for our wedding, initially planning a very small, quiet ceremony. However, Merrie thought that we had best invite all of her relations and friends and all of mine, because, she said, "they all live so far away that they'll be unable to come, but they would like to be invited." So, the invitations went out and we relaxed, waiting for the polite refusals and regrets. We underestimated our own popularity. Everyone invited accepted! Merrie and I had a wedding to organise!

Well, somehow we managed it; I borrowed ten pounds from Merrie for the licence fee. We went to Moss Bros. and hired a suit for me. Merrie made the cheque out to "Moss Broth" and the very dignified assistant softly approached me, holding the cheque delicately between finger and thumb, as if it were something faintly repugnant. "Excuse me, sir," he murmured. "Er . . . isn't this some kind of soup?" he asked, indicating Merrie's mistake. We rushed hither and thither and then all too frequently hither again; somehow eventually all was ready. On the morning of the 20th of February, 1967, a reasonably large number of people gathered at the Cathedral. It was a cold, rainy day, and as we turned into Trafalgar Square, on our way to join them, Jonathon's car slid sideways for a second, and I thought, Ye Gods! Not now! We did get there on time, however, and then had to wait for a while—the bride was a little late.

Merrie walked up the aisle of the Chapel blindingly beautiful in a wedding dress of her own creation. I can still see her now, floating rather than walking, aglow with her own inner radiance. I was sartorially not quite completely ridiculous in a tail-coat and the traditional morning dress; no-one under the age of thirty really looks his best in English morning dress.

In addition to Merrie's uncles and aunts and cousins, her mother, father and brother were there; the only members of the family who were missing were her sister, who still lived in Tasmania at that time, and her elder brother, Stephen, in Hamburg. Merrie and I were married and went to spend a two-day honeymoon at the Park Lane Hotel in Mayfair (two days of that was all we could afford). On the morning of our second day, the telephone rang. The only person who knew our whereabouts was Jean, who was staying at our small flat in North London during our absence to look after Merrie's mother, Ermyn, who was still convalescing after a serious illness which she had contracted in East Africa. She had also broken her leg, and Merrie had flown to Dar es Salaam and brought her back to London, while I had been working as a stable-master at Bertram Mills Circus (and if that seems to be complicated, believe me, it was, and yes, there is a story attached, but it has no place in any further detail in *this* book). Jean was calling to tell us that a telegram had arrived from Australia House asking me to telephone them at once. I promptly did so, and was told that we had been assigned berths on a ship leaving Southampton in less than a month, and would we please finalise our affairs as soon as possible. We rapidly made all the arrangements we could make, the chief difficulty being what to do with Ermyn, who determinedly (and characteristically) refused all invitations and suggestions as to her future put forward by her brother, Sir Edward, and her sister, Ista, and eventually went her own way, but again that is another story; suffice it to say that she arrived in Tasmania before we did.

Merrie had fallen in love with the tall English perambulators (baby carriages) and said that, since they were not available in Australia, we would buy one in London, have it crated and take it with us. That project, we decided, could wait until we had toured around England and said farewell to all our friends and relatives. The most memorable occasion on that journey was when we bade good-bye to the Malet family at Taunton and climbed into the train to Bristol, where we were to change trains to catch an express to London. Merrie cried floods of tears all the way from Taunton to Bristol; every time she tried to tell me why, she simply broke down again. I resolved not to try to talk about whatever it was that had affected her so deeply until she had fully recovered her composure. Changing trains at Bristol quieted her emotions and she was able to tell me that Sir Edward had told her in parting that he had faith in me, and thought that Merrie had chosen wisely and well in her selection of a husband. I have always been grateful to him, for Merrie needed to hear something like that, and I suppose so did I. We travelled from place to place and took our leave of all those for whom we cared and who we felt cared for us: the Price family, whose unfailing kindness to us extends to this day; the Malets, of whom the same can be said; Jean Wakeman, always my ally and support; the Stevens family and many others, tearful farewells for Merrie and solemn partings for me. Then, finally, back to London and the frantic rush to pack everything.

To Harrods we went to buy a pram. We looked at prams

of all shapes, sizes and colours and finally selected one, all white and dark blue, with a Wedgewood-style plaque on the sides. We duly bought it and then I asked that it be crated and at Southampton Docks within five days. The assistant said that was impossible, to which I replied that I thought that for Harrods nothing was impossible. He agreed, and promised that all would be arranged, then, making polite conversation, he asked, "And how long have Mr. and Mrs. Gresham been married?" "About two weeks," I replied. "Oh, ah, yes. Er, quite so." Merrie quickly explained that we wanted the pram now only because there were none of this quality available in Tasmania. (That pram has carried our four children and is now waiting to be passed on to grandchildren.) Finally, we found ourselves at Southampton Docks aboard the small, badly designed ship *Aurelia* of the Cogedar Line out of Taranto. The ship was one of those elderly vessels which astute ship-owners had bought up after the war and had converted to carry as many human cattle as they could hold, then applied to the immigration runs between Australia and the Old World and also between Europe and South America. Passengers were plentiful and government assistance ensured the receipt by the shipping company of fares.

Poor old ship. The *Aurelia* is probably by now moving around various nations of the world as parts of a large number of Japanese cars. She had started her life as a U-boat supply vessel, and it's almost a pity that she had not ended it that way. Crammed from holds to decks with the disillusioned, the ambitious, the fugitive, the hopeful and the hopeless of several nations, she plodded between Australia and Europe, becoming increasingly weary with every turn of her aged shafts.

Merrie shared a cabin with several other girls, while I shared another, at the other end of the ship, with five young Irish labourers. However, we spent every waking minute together. Finally, at Fremantle, we were assigned to our own private cabin, as a large portion of the ship's complement of passengers had disembarked there.

Merrie's reaction to her first sight of those drab, sandy banks which reach out to enfold a ship as it makes its slow, careful way into the Swan River estuary was to burst into tears, for here at last was Australia, the land that for her was home and had been for most of her life. She had left her homeland for a six-month working holiday and was returning nearly four years later, married, and a very different woman from what she had been when she left. We went ashore in Fremantle, as indeed we had at every possible opportunity, and I had my first Australian steak. It was *good!* We re-embarked and moved to our new cabin, and the gallant old vessel struggled out across the Great Austalian Bight. This was the finest part of the voyage for me, for Merrie and I were together at night as well as during the day. We sailed through the edge of a cyclone, and the majority of those passengers remaining on board kept to their cabins in misery. The ship plunged, rolled and gyrated and those of us who were hardy sailors enjoyed it immensely.

We landed at Melbourne and were transported through the drab suburbs of that crushingly boring city, which seemed to be almost entirely comprised of bungalows, out to Essendon airport, and thence we flew to Hobart, the capital city of Tasmania, the island state of Australia which lies about 300 miles south of Melbourne across one of the world's most dangerous stretches of water, the infamous Bass Strait. There, we were met by Merrie's sister Bliss and her husband at the time and taken to their home. They were exceptionally kind to us, but we both longed for solitude in which to enjoy each other's company without the distractions of other people around us, and we soon made plans to explore Tasmania. We bought a second-hand Holden Utility, which Merrie christened "Honk," loaded it with our camping equipment, and set off to look at our chosen home. We slept either in a small tent or in the back of the "ute." I remember well our first night spent in the Tasmanian bush. We stopped as the summer afternoon faded into dusk and selected a place to camp, and there, surrounded by the oily scent of eucalyptus and the smoke of our camp-fire, we settled down for the night. Merrie cooked a meal over the fire while I prepared our bed in the back of the ute by inflating two air mattresses (which made me dizzy). We ate by the fire and drank Boags beer (which made me dizzy) and then retired together to the ute, and the sensation of being so alone, far out in the Tasmanian Forests with the one person in my life with whom I wanted to share that night was one of pure delight. We lay in each other's arms talking softly for a while, the quiet holiness of the forest night bringing our voices to whispers.

I started up in alarm at a sudden series of loud thumps and a crashing noise in the bushes, but Merrie, her eyes glowing in the starlight, amusement in her voice, said, "Don't worry, silly. It's only a wallaby." And so it was.

We drove north on the Lakes Highway, a dirt, dust and rock road which winds its way through the central upland lake district of Tasmania. We arrived at a place called Claude Road and went to visit an old friend of Merrie's family, one Guy Rowell and his wife. Claude Road lies in awe at the foot of the towering grim dignity known as Mount Roland. This huge mass of rock rears itself rather like an affronted schoolmaster high above the surrounding countryside, which is a patchwork of green fields interspersed with the reddish chocolate colour of tilled paddocks, and the mottled darker shades of green which are the areas of bush.

The Rowells invited us to stay for a couple of nights and gave us a room. The day after our arrival there, a party of the Rowells' friends arrived, among them John Anderson, who, on learning that we were looking for a farm, immediately told us of a small 100-acre holding which had recently come onto the market quite near where he managed a large estate, and he suggested that we continue to the north-west of Tasmania and visit his employers, a family called Mackay. These good people at once took us in and gave us the use of their "sleep-out," a building apart from the main house which served as a guest bedroom. We stayed with them for a full fortnight, during which time we went to see, fell in love with, and arranged to purchase "Rivendell Farm," as we decided to call it. We moved to Rivendell several weeks before the scheduled settlement date on the purchase contract and encountered there the first inhospitable Tasmanians I'd met. (I have met very few since.) The house had three bedrooms, but Merrie and I were not invited to share its comforts. We camped in our small tent until the early autumn rains flooded us out, and then we moved into the barn. Finally, the papers were all signed and sealed, and this elderly farmer and his surly wife moved out, and Merrie and I moved in.

Rivendell was a lovely place, and we remained there long enough to have two sons and start a third, but neither Merrie nor I had ever been to any other part of Australia and we still had a certain amount of wanderlust. So when a certain somewhat too clever neighbour decided to take advantage of the "green Pommy" (an inexperienced Englishman) and attempted to acquire our farm at a rock-bottom price by a complicated and rather cunning piece of agricultural-economic skulduggery, he found that, green though I might have been, I was not a complete fool. To his chagrin, he found himself manouevred into a position where his cheapest and safest course of action was to buy the property for far more than it was worth and at a price which gave us a large profit, so large in fact that we were able to buy a large, powerful car and a twenty-four-foot caravan, or house trailer, and still put into the bank considerably more capital than we had started with.

By this time, I had a job at a local radio station as an announcer and we had discovered that Merrie was pregnant with our third son. A friend who had a farm near Burnie, the town in which the radio station, 7BU, was located, offered us a place to park our caravan until the new Gresham had arrived and established him/herself. We lived in our small, compact and comfortable home at what the little ones called "Alboat's place" for almost a year. It is astonishing how fixed and immobile a caravan can begin to seem if it is parked in one spot for long enough. It is amazing also how quickly Merrie will make a home out of the most unlikely places in which she finds herself. Flowers and vegetables seem to spring into existence around her as if the very earth itself welcomes her attentions.

Eventually, in God's good time, Dominick decided to join his two elder brothers, James and Dig (Timothy), and he made his entrance onto the stage of this world playhouse in the customary way, an event accompanied by a quite perceivable earth tremor, rare in Tasmania. Perhaps young "Pickle" is destined for great deeds; the ancient Greeks would have thought so. As soon as Pickle settled in to the business of being a baby, we packed up our belongings, attached the car to the caravan and pulled. Much to our amazement, it moved, and soon the "snailmobile" was heading towards Devonport to catch the ferry across the Bass Strait to the "North Island," Australia.

CHAPTER 23

Mainland Travails

WE WENT to Melbourne and turned left, our intention being to travel until impecuniosity, boredom or disaster brought us to a halt. Then I would search out a job of some kind and earn money whilst we dealt with whatever situation had presented itself. We travelled slowly and steadily through rich citrus land at Mildura, through dairy lands and beef and sheep country, but found Victoria something of a let-down after Tasmania. On to South Australia and Adelaide, a very pretty city as cities go, but Merrie and I had had our fill of cities, and so we went on.

After driving a day or so out of Adelaide, Dominick's health began to cause anxiety to both Merrie and me. He was a gripy baby, and in the fierce heat of the South Australian summer he had begun to dehydrate. We went to find a doctor. The one we found was a rude, egocentric man, with little compassion, less tact and supreme confidence in his own skills, which, in my opinion, was largely unfounded, though I heard that he was an excellent surgeon. His treatment of Pickle was amateurish, to say the least, and finally we sent the baby to the Adelaide Children's Hospital by air. Soon he was fully recovered and back in Merrie's arms. However, all this cost money, and so we settled down for a while in this dry wheat and sheep area.

I drove a truck, operated a jack-hammer and a rock drill, laid gelignite patterns to blast trenches through the oolitic limestone for water pipes and produced and directed a revue for the local theatrical club, all the while attempting to develop a taste for the local beer (I failed). A job on a farm came up and I was soon welding steel cattle yards together. I had never before used a welder in my life, but by the time the boss figured that out, I had become a pretty good welder. The cattle yards finished, the boss asked me to stay on for a while and help generally around the farm. Six months we stayed at this little town, and I became accustomed to riding a horse through the mallee scrub to find and muster a mob of sheep, to the insistent mocking calls of hundreds of pink and gray galah parrots, the air so hot on one occasion that I was holding my breath whenever in sunlight and breathing only when we passed through the shade of a tree. I was amazed to realise that the horse was doing the same thing. Riding out to check on a windmill, chewing on a sour quondong or native wild peach fruit to try to keep my mouth moist, the air searing my nose and lungs, I would watch the huge 'roos basking in the sun or, if I rode too close to them, bounding away with their unique grace and beauty. Arriving at the windmill and its associated tank and trough, I would check the float valve first and then collapse into the tank of green, scummy bore water. Thoroughly wet, I would then check the windmill itself and wet my clothes again before remounting to ride on to the next mill. If the water had green algae scum growing in the tank, the slow trickle from the windmill outlet pipe was probably safe to drink, though it wouldn't taste too good, but if the tank was clear of weeds and bright blue or a rusty colour, the water contained so many salts and minerals that it was unusable to human beings who did not have a cast-iron intestinal tract.

Sheep and cattle and sometimes horses would drink from those wells, and the 'roos loved them. Contrary to popular beliefs, the farming of many areas of Australia has increased the populations of indigenous life forms by providing pastures and water supplies for the herbivores and herbivores for the carnivores. Large areas of the marginal country, on the other hand, have been destroyed by foolish and greedy men who overstock the area. The cattle and sheep eat everything; first the cattle eat the longer grasses and plants and then the sheep eat the rest down to the roots, and, if times are bad, they even dig up the roots. They eat the seedlings of the trees and stand habitually beneath the trees for shade; any seedlings that they don't eat, they tread to death with their sharp hooves. In time, the adult trees mature and die and there are no seedlings to replace them, the grasses and bushes die from over-grazing, and then the cattle and sheep die, for there is nothing left to eat. Then the greedy grazier goes on the dole. I have seen, in inland Australia, thousands of acres of desert studded with dead trees. However, many farmers (I hope most of us) are ardent conservationists in the true sense of the word. Our life and our living is in the soil of this earth and is governed by the climate and the health of that soil. I shoot wallaby and have shot 'roo and possum, not for sport, though I will not pretend that I don't take pride in my skill with weaponry, but to keep the numbers down to a manageable and stable population level, at which the risk of epidemic or famine is negligible and at which some pasture is left for my stock to eat.

When Merrie and I were convinced that Dominick was fully strong enough to face the rigours of our continuing our odyssey, we once again packed our belongings into the car and caravan and bundled James and Dig and Pickle, our three boys, and Rindle, our boxer bitch, into the car and once again I let out the clutch on the snailmobile and we were westward bound. Out towards Ceduna and Penong, and then the dreaded Nullabor Plain. In those days, the Nullabor was a dangerous dirt track, known optimistically as the "Eyre Highway," which stretched away before one, clear off the edge of the world, to lose itself somewhere in the silver-streaked sky of the western horizon. The Nullabor Plain itself is, as its name suggests, almost treeless, being a long, flat area of scrub and desert which, despite itself, holds a weird and hostile beauty. Out on the Nullabor a person is forced to admit his or her insignificance before the face of God. If you stop your car and, taking a careful compass direction, simply walk into the scrub for half an hour in a straight line (following the compass), you will soon discover that out there there is nothing, nothing but you, the desert and He who created it. The desert will not acknowledge you; it doesn't care. The Nullabor is older than we are and will be there long after we are gone. In the history of the Nullabor Plain, the life of mankind is less than the flicker of a firefly's tail, and it just doesn't care. Stand there for a while and breathe the desert air, then follow your reciprocal bearing back to your car and drive away; the Nullabor is still there, but you aren't.

We destroyed seven tyres on that trek, and I seemed to spend all my time jacking up the caravan and changing wheels. Our money, carefully hoarded over the past few months, soon became sadly depleted, as I was forced again and again to pay exorbitant prices for second-hand tyres from profiteers who had set up roadside hovels (they called them "garages") out in the desert. I changed wheels in a sandstorm, which blasted the skin of my torso red raw. I changed wheels at night when the cold made fingers clumsy and numb. I changed wheels in the sun, the sweat running from my armpits and trickling coldly down my sides. I began to long for the West Australian border, for there at Eucla the road was once again a sealed highway. Merrie and I did not quite get out of the car and kiss the tarmac at the border, but we certainly felt like doing so. To be back on a sealed road again was heaven, and, in high spirits, we drove on to Norseman.

The Nullabor had not quite finished with us, however, for by way of a Parthian shot it sent its malevolence into the town after us. We had just pulled into the Norseman Caravan Park and begun to set up for the night when disaster struck the entire town. I was in the caravan with Merrie and the two elder boys, and Pickle was still asleep in his bassinet in the car, when suddenly there was a loud bang, as if someone had thrown a large stone at the van. I looked at Merrie, and she at me. Then there came another report and another, and, with a shattering roar, all hell broke loose. It sounded as if a madman had opened fire on us with a machine gun. Glass from the windows began to explode into the van. I seized the bedclothes from the bed and threw them around Merrie and the boys, pushing them into the sheltered recess of the stove, where they would be shielded by built-in furniture on all sides, for by now I had realised the nature of the assault: a hailstorm. Hailstones the size of golf balls were hurtling down upon us at an angle of forty-five degrees, driven by a maliciously savage desert wind. I grabbed an industrial safety helmet from a cupboard and leapt out of the van to check that Pickle was all right. I was clad only in a pair of shorts and took a sad battering to find my youngest son still fast asleep in his bassinet, blissfully unaware of the cacophonous hammering row on the roof of the car. Rindle the dog was trying to shelter in the still open boot (trunk) of the car, so I shut the lid on her and dashed back to the van, judging that Pickle was safer where he was than he would be anywhere else and, in any case, to try to move him was out of the question. Dizzied by the hammer-blows of the hailstones bouncing off my helmet, I hurled myself into the shelter of the van. The storm lasted only a few minutes, and when it was over, I unfolded my arms from around Merrie and the two boys. Whilst they went outside to romp with delight amongst the piled-up drifts of hailstones, Merrie and I surveyed the damage. One injury only. Flying glass had sliced through the skin of Merrie's thigh, but, although bloody, the wound was not deep and a simple sticky-plaster dressing was sufficient to close it. I was battered and bruised about the chest and shoulders, but otherwise unhurt. All the children, and the dog, were fine. Not so the inanimate members of our party, however. Every window on the starboard side of the van was smashed; the side of the van was pock-marked with small dents. The car, likewise, was covered on its right-hand and upper surfaces with shallow indentations.

Insurance covered almost all the repair work, which we eventually had done in Perth months later. We left Norseman the next morning and drove south to Munglinup. There were two reasons for this diversion to the bottom left-hand corner of the continent. The first was that once again we needed money, and the farmer for whom I had worked in South Australia had a brother-in-law there, who, he told me, was sure to know of any work available in the area; and, second, Harry Malet was managing an estate in that area.

Once again the snail was mobile and we found our destination without a great deal of trouble. The brother-in-law himself gave me a job and at an even better rate of pay than his generous South Australian counterpart had paid. Before long we had replaced the glass in the van and had put a couple of brand-new tyres on it. I worked at a variety of tasks and eventually found myself roustabouting for the shearers and killing a sheep a day for their meat supply (and ours). I enjoyed some of the work and some I loathed. One job which I found particularly disgusting was the task of towing the carcases of the dead sheep away to the swamp every morning before breakfast. The sheep were mustered for shearing too early, and in too large mobs, and so were starving to death in the small holding paddock, but the farmer was not keen on letting them return to feed-rich paddocks, for it would have meant mustering again. He did not really like work.

Working meant income and income meant saving. Soon we had enough money to consider moving on. One fascinating sight I saw whilst in the area was an Aboriginal stockman (what he was doing that far south, I don't know) catching his supper. This black native Australian had two or three highly intelligent dogs, with which he worked the sheep, and (I believe this is unusual) he worked on foot also. One afternoon we were moving a mob of weaners when a large racehorse goanna frightened by the hoofbeats or the general kafuffle suddenly emerged from beneath a bush and, emulating its namesake, headed for the horizon. The old shepherd no sooner saw the creature than he "sooled" his dogs onto it. The dogs drove the lizard, three feet long at least, straight to the old man, who stood as still as a post, as if rooted to the spot upon which his broad bare feet were anchored. The lizard, in its panic, clawed its way up his legs and climbed up his chest and finally came to rest with its front claws gripping his forehead, its rear claws on his shoulders and its tail dangling down his back. It looked around superciliously, as if mocking the dogs who pranced around barking and leaping. The lizard looked one way and then another, turning its foolish head like a monarch surveying a group of peasants. Suddenly, with a movement too quick to be seen, the old man reached up and grabbed it by the neck; one quick, hard twist and the creature expired; as if at a signal, the dogs fell silent and dutifully went back to work around the lambs. Ignoring the deep, bleeding scratches that the claws had left on his body, the old man grinned up at me as I reined in my horse beside him. "Missis gonna be cook 'im up tonight. Good tucker!" he said happily. I knew then, suddenly, that I had met a man who was a part of his environment and who made no effort to batter his world into submission, but merely adapted himself to fit in with it. The Australian Aboriginal tribes are one of the last of the ultra-civilized pre-primitive races to fall beneath the blunt edge of Caucasian proliferation.

We left Munglinup at last and toured round the coastline of the south-west corner of Western Australia. We found ourselves liking that area, because it had a "Hobbity" feel to it and was "almost as nice as Tasmania." Albany, Bunbury and then to Perth. Soon our caravan was parked in the back yard of the house where Mary-Jane Malet, Sir Edward's younger daughter, was living with her husband in the pleasant riverside suburb of Bassendean. I began to look for work, but with little success. Finally, I was offered two widely different jobs, both on the same day and for the same pay. One was a position as the manager of a farrowing unit of a large and intensive piggery; the other was as a staff announcer at a small country radio station at a place called Katanning. The radio job had several factors in its favour, but one of the chief attractions was that a house went with the job. Off to Katanning we went, and I duly started work at 6WB as the only member of the announcing staff who wasn't married to the manager. The three of us got along very well, and Merrie made up a foursome. We also worked well together and became friends, spending a great deal of our spare time together. Merrie had just about finished unpacking the caravan and moving into the house, some weeks later, when the manager of 6IX, the parent station in Perth, drove down one morning to talk to Peter Cooper, the 6WB manager. He told me that he wanted me in Perth the following week to read news for 6IX. That move to Perth began an eight-year stint on radio and television, which culminated in my resignation (in disgust) from the top-heavy bureaucracy of the Australian Broadcasting Commission.

Meanwhile, whilst I was beginning a successful career in the electronic media, far away from the white-fire glare of the West Australian sun, amid the mists and mournful winds of the winter of his life, an old and lonely man was grieving for his memories and waiting apathetically for his own death. I seldom ever thought of him in those days, and he almost never wrote to me. On the rare occasions when he did, his letters tasted of bitterness and reproach and I destroyed them. I didn't even want to think about Warnie.

Whilst I was farming, working, living and learning about life and myself in Australia, Warnie was spending the end years of his allotted time grieving for Jack and living one day to the next very much under the control and sway of the Millers. I am not at all sure that Warnie was not aware of their hopes and that he was not using them as much as they were trying to use him. Walter Hooper visited Warnie on frequent occasions, and Warnie probably felt that Walter liked to exhibit him almost as if he were a living relic, the brother of the great C. S. Lewis. This very American attitude Warnie would have found tasteless and incomprehensible. For much of the time, I believe, Warnie remained sober, but also for much of the time he drank.

Early in 1973 I was alerted by Jean Wakeman to the fact that Warnie was very ill, and I began to arrange to fly back to England. The British Consulate was very helpful and rushed my passport through the various official channels. TVW Ltd., the broadcasting network for which I was working, were also very helpful, allowing me to schedule my holidays for whenever I wished to take them. Then, on the 9th of April, Jean telephoned the studio to tell me that I would be flying to England for a funeral, for Warnie had died. I arrived in London about thirty hours later, after B.O.A.C. had organised for me a seat on the first available flight. I hired a car and drove to Oxford. I was greeted at the back door of The Kilns by Mr. Miller, who met me with the words "Wot d'you want? The car's ours. The Major said the car was to be ours"! He seemed jumpy, nervous and irritable, and no wonder, for he had been found (by the man who told me of it) removing the gold links from the shirt on Warnie's still warm body. Discovered in this action, he had said, "The Major said I was to 'ave these"! The Major said! The Major said! How often, I wonder, did this poor specimen of mankind feel the need to repeat this useless and transparent refrain as a sop to the proddings of his all but quiescent conscience?

Warnie was gone. The Kilns at last passed into the past. I attended Warnie's funeral, but I can remember very little of it except that it took place on a fine, bright spring morning, such as Warnie would have found a delight in its heralding of the coming of summer. When I entered The Kilns itself, I found that it was empty, sacked as thoroughly as if by a band of Viking marauders. Everything was gone; all the furniture, books, paintings. Everything. One artifact remained of all the things of my own which I had left there, naïvely assuming their safety, a soapstone-handled Arabian dagger which Mother had bought for Jack as a present and Jack had passed on to me after Mother's death. The "Calormen Dagger" is a valuable piece, so how it was overlooked in the rape of The Kilns I cannot imagine. It sits on my desk in Tasmania now, and there I hope it will stay.

It was on this visit that I last saw Fred Paxford. As I have related earlier, on my next return to England, some years later, I drove out to the village of Churchill to see him, only to be told that he had died two years earlier, suddenly, whilst sitting in his favourite chair watching television. His neighbours told me that Fred's family had come at once from Chipping-Norton and taken care of all the funeral arrangements and cleared out his rooms. They were followed a day later by a small, twitchy man with a face "like a disappointed rat," who had been livid with rage that the family had beaten him to it. His name? Len Miller.

The Kilns was sold to property developers who, of course, destroyed the property by building ugly houses on every square inch of it possible, where once lovely trees had stood, now stand maisonettes, and thus are the memories of childhood swept away. The wood and the lake have passed into the hands of the Buckinghamshire, Berkshire and Oxfordshire Naturalists Trust, and although for a while they were well cared for, the lake is now, probably through lethargy and shortage of funds, being allowed to silt up. Soon it will disappear altogether, becoming merely a sodden patch of boggy ground; with its passing will go many phantoms.

Men must endure their going hence, but I wish they had not gone.

INDEX